PETRONIUS –

PETRONIUS – THE BOOK

Andrew Lothian

London/Edinburgh
Butterworths/Law Society of Scotland
1988

United Kingdom	Butterworth & Co (Publishers) Ltd, 88 Kingsway, LONDON WC2B 6AB and 4 Hill Street, EDINBURGH EH2 3JZ
Australia	Butterworths Pty Ltd, SYDNEY, MELBOURNE, BRISBANE, ADELAIDE, PERTH, CANBERRA and HOBART
Canada	Butterworths Canada Ltd, TORONTO and VANCOUVER
Ireland	Butterworth (Ireland) Ltd, DUBLIN
Malaysia	Maylayan Law Journal Sdn Bhd, KUALA LUMPUR
New Zealand	Butterworths of New Zealand Ltd, WELLINGTON and AUCKLAND
Singapore	Butterworth & Co (Asia) Pte Ltd, SINGAPORE
USA	Butterworths Legal Publishers, ST PAUL, Minnesota, SEATTLE, Washington, BOSTON, Massachusetts, AUSTIN, Texas and D & S Publishers, CLEARWATER, Florida

All rights reserved. No part of this publication may be reproduced or transmitted in any form or by any means, (including photocopying and recording) without the written permission of the copyright holder except in accordance with the provisions of the Copyright Act 1956 (as amended) or under the terms of a licence issued by the Copyright Licensing Agency Ltd, 33–34 Alfred Place, London, England WC1E 7DP. The written permission of the copyright holder must also be obtained before any part of this publication is stored in a retrieval system of any nature. Applications for the copyright holder's written permission to reproduce, transmit or store in a retrieval system any part of this publication should be addressed to the publisher.

Warning: The doing of an unauthorised act in relation to a copyright work may result in both a civil claim for damages and criminal prosecution.

© Butterworth & Co (Publishers) Ltd 1988

A CIP Catalogue record for this book is available from the British Library.

ISBN 0 406 10396 8

Typeset by Phoenix Photosetting, Chatham, Kent
Printed and bound in Great Britain by
Mackays of Chatham PLC, Chatham, Kent

To ANDY, NICHOLAS, JAMES and ROBERT

Preface

Some twenty years ago, Philip Caplan, then at the top of the junior bar, told me that his friend Alfred Phillips was looking for someone to write a regular piece on matters of cultural and/or humorous interest for *The Journal of the Law Society of Scotland*, which he edited. It was a welcome opportunity. Like many others before and since, I was turning to occasional journalism as a means of supplementing my meagre earnings. When offered the column, I accepted happily, thus laying the foundation for friendships that continue.

There were two immediate problems. First, a *nom de plume* was required, etiquette demanding that an advocate should write for a legal magazine in his own name on legal matters only. While I doubted that my views on, say, mid-period Dylan Thomas would increase my practice in the Valuation Appeals Court, I had to concede that my knowledge of rating law certainly would not either, and accordingly I refrained from any semblance of touting.

As it happened, a few years previously I had come upon and much enjoyed William Arrowsmith's translation of the *Satyricon* – sometimes described as the first novel, later filmed to great effect by Fellini – a fantastical, satirical account of strategies for survival in ancient Rome, written by the man known as *arbiter elegantiae* to the Emperor Nero – adviser on matters of taste to a talented monster. Since two other writers whom I admired greatly had spoken well of him – thus J. K. Huysmans in *Against Nature*: 'depicting in a splendidly wrought style, without affording a single glimpse of the author . . . the vices of a decrepit civilization'; thus Cyril Connolly in *Enemies of Promise*: 'a copy of the *Satyricon* bound in crushed levant and kept in my pew in chapel, where it looked like some solemn book of devotion and was never disturbed' – and since I felt that I would have enjoyed meeting the old boy, I stole his name.

Secondly, there was the problem of finding a first subject that would establish the tone of the column. Here I was lucky. The poet Robert Garioch, whom I knew slightly, had mentioned to me that he had been invited to address a supper somewhere on Burns Night, devoted to the Immortal Memory of James Hogg, the Ettrick Shepherd, who, wishfully, claimed the same birthday as the Bard. Hogg, a very great writer who, when it suited him, could convince people that he was a country buffoon and little more, seemed both cultural and humorous. Thus Hogg was the first subject and I have tried to repay my debt to both writers by mentioning them as often as is decent over the years.

By and large, I have found it more interesting to try to share enthusiasms than to express dislikes. I believe that, thanks to Hugh MacDiarmid, we do have a Scottish literary culture once again, that in Charles Rennie Mackintosh we have an artist whose greatness we are even now only beginning to understand, that if you can show me a better poet than Norman MacCaig I'll give you ten shillings . . . but that's enough of beliefs. My thanks go to Alfred for having the idea, to his successor as editor, Willie Millar, for his confidence in allowing me a free hand, and most of all to David Fletcher, who has been with Petronius from the beginning and who has made and put together this selection. He is always the first to see a new piece. His inventive theories of punctuation and intuitive opinions about what a handwritten word might be have regularly helped me to achieve that combination of shock and surprise that we all strive for. Although I have never dared to stop and think for whom these pieces have been written, if I found out that David didn't like them, then I'd certainly stop and think again.

Andrew Lothian
Glasgow, July 1988

Contents

Preface vii

Unfinished 1
Scots Law on the Small Screen 4
Dirty Deeds 1 7
Dean's Sing-along 9
No Trouble Brewing 12
An April Adoration 15
Spit and Polish 18
The Game of the Name 20
Waxen Images 22
Happy Anti-holidays 25
Highland Village 27
Scots Worthies 29
Playing the Game 31
The Dog Bus Leaves at 5 am 33
A Lacuna in the Palimpsest 36
Bizarre Bazaar 39
The Strange Case of Deacon Brodie 41
Boundless, Endless and Subminimal 44
Pick-pockets of Literature 46
Artists' Visions 49
Second Hand 52
Kay of Edinburgh 55
Dirty Deeds 2 57
Landlord and Tenant 59

Contents

Putting on the Style   61
Distraction   63
Hearts, that Once Beat High   66
Aesthetics and the Finance Committee   68
Cameronian   71
Good Scout   74
Handy Hints for the Man of Letters   77
The Living Dead   80
People's Palaces   83
Wally's Wha Haes   86
Correspondence Course   89
Lucy   92

Unfinished

'FORD, John (1586–1639), English dramatist, four of whose plays are lost, destroyed by Warburton's cook.' In this tantalising way begins the entry on Ford in *The Oxford Companion to the Theatre*. What a vivid scene is thus conjured up: in the kitchen, Ford aghast, Warburton embarrassed and impotent, and the nameless cook flushed with righteous triumph, like some seventeenth-century Muggeridge. Further research, unfortunately, reveals that this is pure fancy. The cook, Betsy Baker, used her antiquarian master's collection of manuscripts for 'putting under pye bottoms' and thus destroyed the plays. For a long time it was not considered that this was much of a loss, but there has been a revival, in recent years, of interest in Jacobean dramatists, and now the loss of any work by the esteemed author of *'Tis Pity She's a Whore* (splendid title) is deeply regretted.

To speculate on the missing and the incomplete in literature is a diverting, and not necessarily fruitless, exercise. F. Scott Fitzgerald died leaving *The Last Tycoon* unfinished, and R. L. Stevenson did the same with *Weir of Hermiston*. Which would we rather have completed? The portrait of Adam Weir, which makes up most of what we do have of the latter book, is Stevenson at his best, but there are signs from his notes that the rest of the story was liable to become blood and thunder and we may be better off with a fragment. Fitzgerald, on the other hand, seemed well on the way to writing another *The Great Gatsby* and his notes reveal that he had already carefully plotted the rest of the book in a way that suggests that what followed would not only develop, but would also modify what had already been written.

If the failure of Fitzgerald and Stevenson to finish their books is sad, much worse is the story of Nikolai Gogol and *Dead Souls*. The first part of this comic masterpiece was published in 1842. Ten years later the author had completed the second part, by which time he had, most unfortunately, fallen under the influence of a fanatical priest, Father Matthew, who ordered him to destroy the manuscript and enter a monastery. Gogol burned the book, and ten days later died.

Books that remain unfinished are generally produced by the accident of death. It seems rare for a writer to do what Schubert apparently did with the Unfinished Symphony, that is to say, put it in a drawer and forget about it. The reason for this is that a writer, if he has sufficient reputation, can usually publish extracts as he goes along, either as part of a work in progress or as individual stories.

As for lost works, it is the ancients that suffer most. For the modern writer, the demand for manuscripts by academic institutions is sufficient to preserve the most trivial jottings, and there is no danger, for instance, that the hoard of Hemingway manuscripts which have just come to light will disappear again, unless someone decides to protect the author's reputation by putting an embargo on what he himself had not thought worthy of publication. On the other hand, we are very lucky to have anything at all of the works of the Roman poet Catullus. Tradition has it that his poems were lost until the end of the thirteenth century, when a copy was discovered, somewhat stained, wedging a wine barrel in Verona. This copy was eventually lost again, and since then scholars have been kept busy trying to reconcile the various inaccurate copies made of that copy.

It is in the nature of something that is lost that we are not likely to know what it was. There is, however, at least one lost work that we do know something about. The fragment we have is a licentious, witty account of two of the least noble Romans in literature as they wander through the feasts, amphitheatres, markets and brothels of Imperial Rome. The eternal follies are mocked with a sharp gaiety that makes one long, in vain, for more. We have the fifteenth and sixteenth books, and the hope is that some day, somewhere, the rest will turn up. The book is the *Satyricon*, and the author, the *arbiter elegantiae* of Nero's court, is Petronius.

November 1969

Norman MacCaig has been publishing witty, surprising and satisfying poems for so long now that I suspect that we are beginning to take him for granted. 'Good old Norman,' say the selectors, as they consider the Poets' 1st XV. 'You can always rely on him for a good sound image, different but somehow still the same. Reassuring, really.'. . .

Old Maps and New contains poems from all ten collections which Mr MacCaig has published since 1955. Insofar as such things are worth noting, there has been some development in his style. At first he wrote fairly strictly, keeping to regular metre and rhyme. In the late sixties he began to experiment with free verse, or rather found that poems were coming to him in free form. In a way this did not make as much difference to his work as one might have expected: his search for the accurate, indeed the only, word for a particular place in a particular poem has scarcely diminished. What the free form has made possible, however, is for Mr MacCaig to give vent in his work to his particularly mordant brand of humour. The sort of wit which enlivens his conversation now began to appear in his poetry. (He once—or twice—described finishing a novel by C. P. Snow as like coming out of a thin shower of dandruff, unenlivened by even the slightest flash of mediocrity.) Not that his work lacked humour before. Take, for instance, the last two lines of his poem on people looking at Henry Moore's sculptures in the Botanic Gardens in Edinburgh:

'See them, ferocious ratepayers
Flirting with lovely dinosaurs.'

Here the half-rhyme is used to let the short poem make its point succinctly. Free verse, however, allows him to deploy his wit in a more discursive manner, as in 'Wild Oats', about the pigeons outside his window:

'Last week a stranger joined them, a snowwhite pouting fantail,
Mae West in the Women's Guild.'

April 1979
(The Henry Moore sculptures are now less pleasingly displayed in the grounds of the Scottish National Gallery of Modern Art—Editor.)

Scots Law on the Small Screen

The announcement that commercial television schedules for next year include a series built round the incomparable Iain Cuthbertson and entitled *Sutherland's Law* fills one with a chilly anticipation of more than one evening of fury and delight. Mr Cuthbertson's break-through, in terms of television, came comparatively recently, when he followed his successful portrayal of the saintly Dr Arnold in *Tom Brown's Schooldays* with an equally successful portrayal of Charlie Endells, expatriate Scottish pornographer, in *Budgie*. The latter was a series designed to reveal the talents of the former pop singer Adam Faith in the part of an eternally optimistic, eternally useless small-time crook. While Mr Faith was winning polite applause, Charlie Endells Appreciation Societies were springing up in universities and other places of learning in a spontaneous tribute to the sleaziest Scotsman to reach the Big Smoke since James Boswell knocked on Dr Johnson's front door.

Sutherland's Law is to be the tale of a procurator fiscal in Dungarvan, a town recognisable as Oban. The series was given a trial run earlier this year, with a single episode being broadcast to test consumer reaction to the product. Although the plot was screamingly implausible, the court-room scenes avoided many of the errors one has come to accept as normal. At least the sheriff did not have on a full-bottomed wig and the defence counsel did not seem to be wearing a fall and a white bow tie both at once. The sheriff, indeed, was played with a sleepy irascibility and

Gary Cooper-like brevity of utterance that will surely have a few of Her Majesty's judges gazing in the mirror and muttering 'Could it be me?' The principal departure from the normal rules of court-room practice seemed to be the absence of any right of the defence to cross-examine prosecution witnesses, which will presumably help the series create a situation of wish-fulfilment among members of the Fiscal Service.

What one did rather shudder at was the fact that the series appeared to have been cast exactly in the mould of *Dr Finlay's Casebook*. The situation is of a young depute fiscal, full of idealism and enthusiasm and having a nodding acquaintance with modern theories of penology, being thrust into a small town where the fiscal has been running things since the days of Madeleine Smith with only a first edition of *Renton and Brown* to temper his native sagacity and cunning.

The conflict between these rather basic personalities came out in the trial run in a dispute over a fatal accident inquiry—did he fall or was he pushed?—and a draw was generously agreed to be a fair result. No doubt the personalities will continue to clash like dustbins in a gale as we are treated to the panorama of rape, deforcement of messengers, setting fire to naval dockyards, sheep stealing, post office hold-ups, piracy on the high seas, procuring, committing of public nuisances and tourists falling off the pier, that is everyday life in a town such as Oban. Highland policemen will push back their hats and scratch their foreheads, trawlermen in big jerseys and wellies with the tops turned over will drink too much and cast dark looks in public bars, aproned landladies will confess, wise after the event, that perhaps there was something a wee bit odd about the man in number ten (no offence, Mr Heath) and tinkers' encampments will be found to have vanished overnight, with only a circle of burned earth to show where the caravans stood.

The notion of Mr Cuthbertson, whose talents clearly include a lively sense of the absurd, wading thigh-deep in this sea of cliché is highly attractive and should let us see television doing what it does best, which is not to instruct, inform or entertain but to divert from the follies of the world for a short time through the creation of even greater follies.

No doubt the series already has a legal adviser to tell the producer how many go on a jury and what colour of wig a sheriff wears. On the other hand, it may be that the Scottish legal profession can make a significant contribution by suggesting suitable stories. These, presumably, should be of a moral and improving nature, so that apart from being to the general enjoyment, they could also have an educational value. For instance, what about a cautionary tale in which the case against an accused is found not proven because the fiscal keeps asking leading questions?

December 1972

The machinery of beer-making can be as complex as you like. Thermometers and hydrometers have their place, but the only essential item is a plastic dustbin. This is filled with malt, hops, water, sugar and yeast in various quantities. After that, nature, red in tooth and claw, takes its course and something drinkable appears in about three weeks' time. What goes on in the bottle I do not yet understand and cannot predict. One bottle will yield a liquid gentle as milk, its brother something ferociously intoxicating. With practice, homogeneity can be achieved. I know a man who can get all his bottles the same, but cannot tell in advance what the strength will be. He has devised a novel test, which consists of drinking a half-pint, playing the first of Bach's forty-eight Preludes and Fugues on his piano, and so on till he has to stop.

For anyone who wants a good home brew, Robert Garioch, in one of his Saxteen Edinburgh Sonnets, gives a workable recipe which ends:

'Fowre days of stishy, and the rocks will sink,
bottle, and keep till clear as cairngorm,
syne cannily, and wi' wyce judgement, drink.'

March 1970

Dirty Deeds 1

Mr Ernest Hemingway Revokes

You know how it is in lawyers' offices in the early morning, before the cleaners arrive. The rain slanting off the window and the thick dust lying in pools and the eager young conveyancing clerks fingering the *Encyclopaedia of Styles* and looking pretty damn legal at that.

The old one put down his pen and looked at the client.

'We could endorse a codicil,' he said.

'I do not like the thing with the codicils,' said the client. 'They are neither tragical nor comical. Therefore they are foolish.'

'Sometimes they are all three,' said the cashier.

'I obscenity in the obscenity of thy obscenity,' said the client.

The old one opened his hide briefcase and shut it again and dropped some papers on the floor. He did not try to pick up the papers. He thought instead of a summer day in '06, with the questions neat and black and white on the examination paper and the answers pouring out onto the page like the bulls of Miura when they run through the streets at the fiesta at Pamplona.

'If you do not like the thing with the codicils, then we will prepare a fresh deed, of course.' Suddenly he felt tired. Once he could have disinherited an entire dynasty before breakfast, as the client sitting in front of him waited.

'You wish to leave something to your family?' he asked hopefully.

'Nothing. Nothing and again nothing.'

'There is the thing with the intestate succession,' he said.

God, let him say 'yes', he thought. He could see the deed of revocation all big and shiny and the words just running to the edge of the paper and the testing-clause with the signature of the client and the signatures of Samantha Macglumph and Senga Mactumph, typists, witnesses.

'I do not like the thing with the intestate succession,' said the client. 'A big deed, disinheriting them all of everything.'

The old one thought of the white farmhouse set across the river and into the trees.

'Even the house of your father?' he asked.

'Go to hell,' said the client. He had decided the night before that he would fire the old one. The old one's nerve had gone, the way that Chicuelito's nerve went after the giant Miura bull caught him against the *barrera* at La Linea while the crowd threw down cushions and empty wine bottles. Once the nerve goes it is hopeless. Sometimes when we heal we are stronger in the broken places, but not once the nerve goes.

'You cannot fire me, because I quit,' said the old one.

'Good,' said the client. He did not like the thing with the multiplepoinding.

October 1979

Next on the list [of buildings which should be demolished], even at the risk of being suspected of a pathological hatred of tall pointed buildings, would be the Scott Monument, were it not that it gives rise to pleasing fantasies that it is in reality a neo-Gothic spaceship, all ready to make Sir Walter the first advocate to reach the moon. In the event of the engines of this monstrous vehicle failing to function at full blast, the voyage would probably end, ingloriously, in the top floor of Messrs Jenners.

January 1969

Dean's Sing-along

Professor Petronius, of the Chair of Applied Application at the University of Bruichladdich, heard Dean Martin on the radio the other morning while eating his birchermuesli and reading the Cambridge Shakespeare. The following notes, pencilled on the business section of *The Sunday Times,* although perhaps lacking that intellectual sharpness which characterised the very best of the Sage of Islay, represent the last of his academic exercises, he having choked shortly thereafter on a fragment of boiled egg.

1 *'I'm praying for rain in California'*

An odd opening. Praying for rain suggests the Indian medicine-man with his primitive belief that the forces of nature could be controlled by human aspiration. The recent upsurge of interest among young Americans in the history of the Red Man is yet another example of the way in which that country persistently redefines itself in terms of its short history. At first sight, it seems perverse that the narrator should be trying to afflict California, which has the reputation of enjoying the best climate in the continent, with bad weather.

2 *'So the grapes can grow and they can make more wine'*

The narrator's intention is now revealed as a beneficent one. Subsequently he is demonstrated to be an unfortunate alcoholic, but it argues a measure of self-control that he should be planning ahead in terms of years rather than of drinks. The viniculture of California, according to Allan Sichel, dates only from the early nineteenth century, 'when missionaries, political refugees, disappointed gold prospectors and immigrants of all kinds from European countries imported their native vines'. Thus we have a paradigm of the American dilemma, the racial melting-pot, the vanishing frontier, the Jamesian *rapprochement* of the innocence of the New World and the experience of the Old. Further, of the many ways of beginning a work of art, the author has chosen a particularly modern one. The ancients, for example, would begin with a brief statement of the author's purpose, such as 'Arms and the man I sing . . .' or 'Of man's first disobedience and the fruit . . .'. In time this developed into epigram form, both covering the subject-matter to come and capable of standing on its own, as in Miss Austen's 'It is a truth universally acknowledged, that a single man in possession of a good fortune, must be in want of a wife.' To begin in a way which is deliberately tantalising, as here, is to make a determined effort not to lose the interest of a fickle audience, as in Norman Mailer's 'I met Jack Kennedy in November 1946. We were both war heroes, and both of us had just been elected to Congress. We went out one night on a double date. . . .'

3 *'And I'm sitting in a honky in Chicago'*

The narrator now appears and we are reminded, by an almost Miltonic use of proper names (cf, 'Jousted in Aspramont or Montalban, Damasco, or Marocco, or Trebisond . . .'), of the breadth of the country as well as the contrast between the golden new California and the bad old gangsterland of Chicago, where the narrator sits enjoying the sunshine in bottled form.

4 *'With a woman and a worry on my mind'*

Nothing useful can be said about this line.

5 *'I ask the man behind the bar to play the juke-box'*

Dean's Sing-along

6 *'And the music takes me back to Tennessee'*

While the sordid nature of the narrator's predicament leads one at the outset to suppose this to be a reference to Tennessee Williams, that darkly effete master of decadence and defeat, it is clear on reflection that it is the state which is intended. The line which we have drawn across the country now plunges south into the lands of nostalgia. While the music in question might possibly be Chuck Berry's rock'n'roll classic, 'Long-distance information, give me Memphis, Tennessee, there's a certain party there who wants to get in touch with me . . .', it is more likely that the reference is to country-and-western music, much of which is created in Nashville, Tennessee, and is of a suitable emetic, not to say carminative, nature.

7 *'And if they ask, who's that fool in the corner, crying?'*

The expanse of the continent, with all the diversity which that implies, has now shrunk to a tiny area of grief, from which the narrator, summoning his last reserves of rueful humour, makes the splendidly vanquished reply which gives the song its title:

8 *'Say it's little old wine-drinker me.'*

December 1974

It seems to me remarkable now that I have read all the major novels of Dostoyevsky. Whatever happened to the intellectual curiosity necessary to do this, and why, at the age of twenty, wasn't I doing something else? The books are there, though, tattered and splattered with coffee stains and suntan oil. They are not replaceable.

March 1985

No Trouble Brewing

Poverty, that enigmatic goddess! Poverty, which drives us to six or seven paperbacks instead of a calf-bound Pascal, to ten days on the Costa Brava instead of a week-end at Gleneagles, to shopfuls of shoes with genuine imitation-leather uppers instead of one pair of Veldskoen of the sort which survived twenty years under water as displayed in a tank in a shop window in South Street, St Andrews, first seen by me in the bucket-and-spade days and still there when I graduated. (Dear me, this is beginning to sound like Jack Kerouac.) Poverty has struck closer to home than ever. It's the drink—home-brewing, and wine-making—or how to make it, much cheaper, and enjoy it so much that the eventual consumption erodes the net savings. But think of the pleasure of living in a house that smells like a shebeen.

Beer is quite easy to make. The only large piece of equipment needed is a plastic dustbin. The thought occurred to me the other night, as a friend's home-brew slipped easily round the teeth and down the throat, that if he could do this with that simple implement, why does the product of a scientific, highly capitalised conglomerate (you name it) taste like the contents of a bowl in which two goldfish have spent someone else's summer holidays? Economies of scale, one assumes.

For some people, the drawback about home-brew is that you have to drink it in someone's home, rather than in the sophisticated or trendy, bleak or squalid atmosphere of a place of public resort. To the pubophile, beer is only one of the considerations. In addition there is the charm of watching the passage of customers, of seeing the business clientele nipping in for a quick one for the road, then followed by the evening's usual customers, those who have already had their tea, and finally the late-comers in for a glass after the theatre or while ostensibly taking the dog for a stroll. There is the charm of pub-talk, of pub architecture, of the friendly barmaid. On the other hand, most pubs are so frightful in every respect—dirty, unimaginative, uncomfortable and unfriendly, disfigured by the ubiquitous television and dispensing badly kept beer and exorbitantly priced spirits—that it is no wonder that increasing numbers of tipplers prefer to stay at home with their heads in their own dustbins.

Times being what they are, it is unlikely that the government would be willing to forgo the excise duty which it gets through the prohibition of home-distilling. Spirits might also be dangerous if not made with care. It occurs to me, however, that anyone with a reasonable knowledge of chemistry should be able to comprehend the principles of distilling. Since the government seems quite unable to work out a way of paying decent wages to doctors and nurses, what about allowing members of the medical profession to make and sell spirits as a means of augmenting their incomes? I suppose it would mean that the surgeries would be packed with revellers, but most doctors are reasonable men of good sense and would no doubt be able to work out some system of separating the prescriptions from the potations.

In terms of the necessary skill to make it, and its alcoholic strength, wine comes between beer and spirits. The practical drawback in the past has been that the stuff takes so long to mature that in order to have an ongoing situation wine-wise you'd need considerably more room than the average home-chemist can afford, and indeed for flat-dwellers it has been suggested that the weight of eighteen months' supply at various stages of development would severely endanger the floors. There is available at least one kit which attempts to avoid this dilemma by promising something drinkable within three weeks of starting. This outfit, which is Danish (Danish Bordeaux?), produces thirty-three bottles for about £6—which is a reasonable price. The lot which I made, though still improving, is best described as certainly wine but not quite normal.

The secret, basically, is that the chemicals which the wine produces during the period of maturation can be added in liquid form at the right moment in order to speed things up. I've tried apple and elderberry so far with excellent results at around 20p per bottle. Long live Poverty.

April 1977

Received ideas

Little Grebe and Little Auk
Two very unfunny small clowns with Chipperfield's Circus around 1950. Their 'Krazy Komedy Kar' frightened those whom it did not depress.

Great Northern Diver
A boastful type found flashing his money in the bars of Peterhead, recognised by his gold jewellery and habit of pressing Rolex watches on comparative strangers. Capable of sinking to considerable depths to find company, especially after dark.

Salad Burnet
Scottish market gardener and health-food faddist. His poem 'To a Turnip', a set of sub-Burnsian stanzas, enjoyed some popularity in its day and was set to music by Sir Arthur Sullivan.

Deathshead Hawkmoth
Devon-born privateer who sailed with Flint and was responsible for introducing cricket to the West Indies after the Sack of Tortuga in 1697. His use of the shinbones of dismissed batsmen as stumps has gone some way towards giving a historical justification to the fast-bowling theories of Clive Lloyd.

June 1986

An April Adoration

'Whanne that Aprille with his shoures sote
The droghte of Marche hath perced to the rote'—
so begins the first bestseller, *The Canterbury Tales*. Chaucer, as usual, was instinctively correct in choosing that particular month to set the tone for his poem: while it would have to be April if the pilgrimage were an Easter one, it was still cunning of him to get the word in so early. Since then, April has been a much-written-about month.

Musicians have been very fond of the month. Al Jolson liked 'April Showers'; the boppers' national anthem was, virtually, 'I'll Remember April', taken at a ferocious speed, which, unusually, made the melody seem more interesting, and everyone likes 'April in Paris'. (A St Andrews University panto about football and witchcraft in the Western Isles had for its overture 'April in Harris'.) Pat Boone, the sanitised rocker, had a hit with the soppy 'April Love' ('is for the very young') and there was a pretty ballad, 'April, Give Me One More Day' ('and she'll be mine in May'), which is not much heard now.

One Sir William Watson, not knighted for his services to literature, it is assumed[1] was responsible for

'April, April,
Laugh thy girlish laughter;
Then, the moment after,
Weep thy girlish tears!'

This, the sort of thing that gets poetry a bad name, reminded me that when Ms Ashley, formerly George something, merchant seaman, re-emerged as a lovely middle-aged lady, the Christian name which she chose was April. Her autobiography, written with Duncan Fallowell, is recommended.

T. S. Eliot had a different attitude to April. He said, at the beginning of *The Waste Land*, that it was the cruellest month, 'stirring dull roots with spring rain', a remark that tells us more about him than it. What he seems to suggest is that winter, where there is no growth or change, is at least static, whereas spring necessitates a response to increasing warmth and light.

Earlier, Robert Browning, in 'Home Thoughts from Abroad', had committed the lines

'Oh, to be in England
Now that April's there',

a fairly banal beginning if ever there was one. The poem improves rapidly, though, and includes one of his finest coinings:

'That's the wise thrush; he sings each song twice over
Lest you should think he never could recapture
That first fine careless rapture!'

Another bird associated with April is the gowk, or cuckoo, the hunting of which was the old Scots equivalent of playing April Fools' Day tricks (the French call it April Fish, apparently). According to Brewer, the day is a vague relic of the Roman feast of Cerealia, which celebrates the capture of Proserpina by Pluto in the Elysian fields and the hopeless search for her by her mother Ceres, pursuing 'the echo of a scream' or the call of the cuckoo.

April, in verse, tends to stand both for freshness and for changeability. As so often, it was Shakespeare (in the little-considered *Two Gentlemen of Verona*) who got the balance just right:

'O! how this spring of love resembleth
The uncertain glory of an April day,
Which now shows all the beauty of the sun,
And by and by a cloud takes all away.'

An April Adoration

An April-gentleman, according to the OED, unfortunately without explanatory notes, is a newly married husband—trying to beat the end of the tax year, presumably, although the usage seems to be one that pre-dates the more demanding incursions of the Revenue. The same page of the dictionary, in conclusion, gives us a word which, one hopes, will soon be back in general parlance. 'To apricate', though rarely used, means 'to bask in the sun'.

April 1985

[1 Apparently he was—in 1917. He was a candidate for the position of Poet Laureate in 1913—Editor.]

Some books for Christmas

For your hip auntie
Mailer by Peter Manso. This fat book of high-class gossip by the likes of Allen Ginsberg, James Baldwin, Shelley Winters, *et al* (many *al*) will probably tell you more about Norman than you actually want to know. The bit on p 485 when Rip Torn tries to hit him on the head with a hammer is particularly good. This is a vastly entertaining book about a man in all senses extravagant. Everyone is so competitive that it is not surprising to find that the most appealing of Norman's many pals is the boxer José Torres. Almost everything about this book is so surprising that it is easy to pick it up for a minute and hard to put it down an hour later. The Naked and the Dead go bananas.

For any social worker (or client thereof)
Witchcraft and Sorcery, edited by Max Warwick.

For lawyers' leisure
Cannibalism and the Common Law, A. W. Brian Simpson. When in 1884 Tom Dudley and Edwin Stephens killed and ate their shipmate, there followed an extraordinary trial for murder in which the defence was one of necessity by custom of the sea. This account of the affair by Professor Simpson is discursive in the extreme, which is no bad thing considering that the author is dealing with subjects as mysterious as sailing ships and the Court of Kings Bench. Some of the Professor's asides: '. . . best known as a criminal practitioner—where purely legal ability is hardly required . . .' may cause mirth. This is a good read in the grand manner: intelligent, lively and enthralling.

November 1986

Spit and Polish

'Bashfulness is the distinguishing characteristic of the English booby, who appears frightened out of his wits if people of fashion speak to him, and blushes and stammers without being able to give a proper answer; by which means he becomes truly ridiculous from the groundless fear of being laughed at.' Sound advice and still apposite, although some two hundred years have passed since it was proffered by Lord Chesterfield in his letters to his son. His son was what is politely known as 'natural', but rather than disown him because of this, the Earl clearly felt obliged to instruct him in honour, virtue, taste and fashion so that, although illegitimate, he would be a credit to his father.

Chesterfield—wit and statesman—was an intimate of Swift and Pope, and his writing has much of the elegant precision of his time, tempered, in the circumstances, with some patience in explaining the rules of the social game. What comes through his advice most strongly today is how closely he identified style with content, like the good Augustan he was.

The copy at which I am looking as I write is, I think, a second edition. It is dated MDCCXCIII, at which time the advice would no doubt be regarded in Chesterfield's own circle as rather outmoded. The volume is designed, by size, for carrying in the pocket, and it may well be that Nathaniel Grieve, the first owner, who has twice signed his name in dark-brown ink, took it with him on his first tentative steps into whatever social world he inclined to. 'Every INSTRUCTION necessary to FORM a MAN of

HONOUR, VIRTUE, TASTE, AND FASHION' says the fly-leaf, and it was one such instruction that first caught my wandering attention: 'Spitting on the floor or carpet is a filthy practice, one which, were it to become general, would render it necessary to change the carpet and the table-cloths.' And on the same page: 'Eating soup with your nose in your plate is also vulgar. So likewise is smelling to the meat while on the fork.' What can they have been like, these gatherings of Englishmen, all intent on exhibiting the very form of the man of honour, etc, consciously eschewing spitting on the floor and smelling the soup? And, if the other warnings are anything to go by, they were liable to seize people by the buttons in order to be heard out, pick their noses while being spoken to, and to burst out with unsuitable mirth at the sight of 'a man's going to sit down in the supposition that he had a chair behind him, and falling down upon his breech for want of one'.

I like to think of them as people who were highly conscious of thesis and antithesis, like the lines of Pope's poetry, where each idea begets its opposite, where the glittering achievements of intellect and fashion form a counterpoint to the acknowledged darkness of a world in which squalor and pain become more unbearable as scientific discovery makes them less incurable.

There was a stylishness about these people which the lumpy Victorians lacked, and there was an acceptance of the body and its needs which the later era refused to allow. Consider whether any Victorian paterfamilias would have advised his son to follow the example of one man who, reluctant to waste a moment and conscious that much poetry could be appreciated in small quantities, bought a cheap edition of Horace and tore out a couple of pages each time he went to his closet, where having read them for some six or seven minutes, he dedicated them to the goddess Cloacina.

Whether or not the son profited much by the advice no one seems to know. One of the few incidents recorded tells us that, having sat down to a laden dinner-table and tucked in what he thought was his napkin, he jumped up on hearing a dog bark and discovered, too late, that it was a corner of the table-cloth. No doubt on that occasion at least he spat on the floor.

November 1977

The Game of the Name

As some celebrity remarked the other day (celebrity = person famous for being famous), 'Whatever happened to the autograph book?' He was not complaining that people had stopped approaching him in restaurants as he and his personal assistant tucked into the lobster thermidor, interrupting a tender moment with a cry of 'Put your John Henry here, squire'. No, what bothered him was that instead of being offered a leatherette oblong with pastel pages, the thing that accompanied a request coupled with the words 'It's for my niece; personally I prefer Mary Marquis' was no more than a scrap of paper.

Now, one can see some advantages for the celebrity in this. If he had time to thumb through a proffered volume, for example, what a blow to his self-esteem might lie there. Put yourself in his position: the choice is a personal one, but would you rather see that your previous co-signatories were Jimmy Savile, Barbara Cartland and James Burke or David Hockney, Sir John Gielgud and the President of the Law Society of Scotland? (Answers on a postcard, please.)

Fired by enthusiasm, I searched out my old book. Autograph hunters were a competitive species: my natural competitor was, naturally, my younger brother. Being a child of some inventiveness and rather shy into the bargain, he hit on the sly scheme of autograph-hunting by post. He would scan the Glasgow evening papers to see who was playing in variety that week, then write to them care of the stage door. In this way, he bagged *inter alia* Jimmy Edwards, Dr Crock (of Dr Crock and His Crackpots, a band we longed to see) and, I think, an early example of a Jimmy Logan. Much as I admired the ploy, I thought it wrong to adopt it, the other chap's idea and all that, but I weakened once and in return got a lovely little self-caricature drawn by Joyce Grenfell.

This second-hand collecting could be valuable. A relative in Blackpool was able to come up with the whole of the team that won the FA Cup in 1953, and that included the immortal Stanley Matthews. My parents once came home from a dinner with the signature of a man who had something to do with The McFlannels. I'd never heard of him at the time, but I followed his subsequent career with interest, right up to his death, as if I had some right of property in him. That sort of thing, though, was an incidental benefit: the real challenge was the direct approach.

The last time I asked for an autograph was when Woody Herman's band played in Glasgow about twenty years ago: they were very gracious, which was reassuring. Prior to that the book is cluttered up with things like Scottish Amateur Tennis runners-up, school friends ('By hook or by crook, I'll be first in your book'—'Did you ever discover you could write on the cover?'), myself, repeatedly, and some names that I cannot put a face to. The great day, however, was when the circus came to town, and in those days the circus meant Bertram Mills. As I look at their names, I can still see Rudy Horn on his unicycle catching plates on the end of a long wand, and the clown Coco, whose fame I could not comprehend, since he never did what I thought a clown should: he never made anyone laugh. Nicest of all in some ways is the childish scribble of one of those lesser characters which the circus attracts: not a star but one of those who help the stars to shine. 'Sheena Ramsay', it says, then in brackets, lest it be forgotten, 'Drum Maggorette' (*sic*).

March 1981

Waxen Images

Visitors to Edinburgh this summer will find something new to look at in the Royal Mile. Among the pubs and tartan shops has appeared the Edinburgh Wax Museum, a diverting and informative institution which looks like being very popular. This is not the first such museum to open in Edinburgh; indeed, as we are told in David Angus's literate guidebook, Madame Tussaud herself took rooms in Thistle Street in 1803, long before she set up her permanent exhibition in Baker Street, London. The last wax museum in Edinburgh (which, incidentally, makes a passing appearance in Sydney Goodsir Smith's great poem 'Under the Eildon Tree'—referred to there as the 'Museum o' Monstrosities') closed in 1939.

The pleasures of waxwork shows are various, although it is doubtful if more pleasure is to be got out of contemplating a good likeness than out of failing to recognise a bad one. Misled by the presence of an apparent corpse on the floor, for example, I identified as Madeleine Smith a lady who turned out to be the wife of Sir James Young Simpson contemplating the first effects of the discovery of chloroform. What is especially interesting is the selection of characters whom the organisers think representative of Scotland's history.

From this selection, there is no doubt that Mary Queen of Scots is seen as the most appealing figure. She features in five tableaux, the best of which is a rather dramatic depiction of the blown-up Darnley lying in the snow outside Kirk o' Field. There is one scene of her with her head on the block, executioner at the ready, which might be thought strong stuff for tiny visitors, but the only childish comment I heard was 'What a clean neck'. Up to the time of Mary, 'History' is represented by Macbeth, Wallace, Bruce and St Margaret. No doubt reasons of space are involved, but the absence of Picts, Romans, St Columba and Vikings looting seems a pity. The Union of the Crowns is represented by a nicely repulsive James VI, but the Union of Parliaments goes unmarked. It occurred to me that it might have been an idea to take Sir Walter Scott out of the montage of 'The Golden Age' (Adam Smith, David Hume, Raeburn, Adam, etc—a dull-looking lot) in order to set him up welcoming George IV on his historic visit to Edinburgh in 1822, a visit which marked the first time that a reigning monarch had been in Scotland for 171 years.

Judging by the exhibition, the twentieth century in Scotland has been somewhat curious. It is a pity that for representative writers, for example, they have not been able to do better than Buchan, Barrie and Conan Doyle, although one is bound to admit that a waxwork of Hugh MacDiarmid would be something of a contradiction in terms. An even more surprising thing, however, considering the national obsession with sport, is the absence of any sportsman at all (except for Captain M. Phillips, who is there for another reason). While the choice of a football or rugby player might have been difficult in view of the vast numbers of both, one would have thought that the boxers Benny Lynch and Ken Buchanan had a good claim to representation (better, say, than Lulu or Ronnie Corbett, admirable as they are), and the fact that, in the homeland of the game, no golfer is represented is odd.

Finally, yes, there is a Chamber of Horrors, covering the ground pretty well. It is a matter of national pride that a little country like ours has produced Burke and Hare, the murdering bodysnatchers, Major Weir the Wizard, Sawney Bean and his cannibal family, and Deacon Brodie, specialist in local government and housebreaking. An addition which I would suggest, as an example of high-class treachery, is the 'Black Dinner' in Edinburgh Castle in 1440 when the Earl of Douglas and his brother were lured to their deaths on a promise of hospitality in an incident commemorated in the contemporary rhyme 'Edinburgh Castle, Toune and Towre/God grant thou sink of sinne,/And that even for the black dinoir/Earl Douglas gat therein'. The Horrors are, of course, all good, nasty fun, but one thing did make me feel a little uneasy and that was the presence there of the murderer Peter Manuel, who was hanged at Barlinnie Prison in 1958. If evil lives are to be used as objects of entertainment, it is reasonable that a little longer than this should go by.

May 1976

Imagine the pure thrill when into the letter box came—inside a magazine that I buy and pay to have sent by post—an unsolicited leaflet soliciting me to join the Poetry Book Society. (When I was a chiseller we had a Poetry Book at the skule. 'And shall Trelawney die?', 'Flow gently, sweet Afton' and all that class of stuff left me cold then—but this was clearly something designed to be more warming.) But the thrill soon turned to chill, for I found myself confronted with the most curious set of contradictions since the Thuggee Society set themselves up as tourist guides. The first thing you get if you join is a selection of 'a number of new works deserving special attention'. (Get that use of 'special'—not just ordinary attention but special. This couldn't be the same fella doing the writing here as used to do the menus for gourmet suppers in the back bar of Murphy's in Ballinasloe—'Dawn-picked mushrooms marinaded in best Swedish claret'—all that class of stuff.) Never mind, we've all selected things in our time and no shame attaching. Each new book Salman Rushdie puts out, for instance, I give special attention to and shout 'Rubbish', and I'm not a hundred per cent sure about John le Carré either, but I don't go putting pamphlets about it through people's doors. What's this next, though? Offers them to members at well below the retail price. That's rich. A promising young versifier is identified and his publisher, taking no end of financial risk with little prospect of reward, is promptly cajoled into undercutting himself. No wonder they say that there's no money in poetry, if 'Everyone Who Enjoys Reading' is getting the stuff at a discount.

April 1988

Happy Anti-holidays

I was discussing the Scottish language with a student thereof the other day. 'Have you ever considered the way Scots use the word "Need"?' he said. 'To give you an example, my father used to say to me, "What you need is a good kick on the backside." What he meant, of course, was that what *he* needed was to give me a good kick on the backside.' 'What about "Belong"?' I replied. 'The use of which I am thinking is similarly reversed, as when a person says "I belong to that", meaning, of course, "I own that."'

Before I could go on with the exegesis, namely that the person is subconsciously admitting, apparently in the face of the rules of grammar, that he is, in the *bourgeois* sense, defined in terms of his possessions, and thus may truly be said to belong to them, the attention of the symposium was distracted by the more immediate need of obtaining further liquid refreshment and the matter was not proceeded with. Perhaps that was as well, for every recourse to the maxim *In vino veritas* is well met by the words of the immortal Flann O'Brien, author of *At Swim-Two-Birds*, that 'your syllogism is fallacious, being based on licensed premises'. Well, thinking is thirsty work, and it was not until later it occurred that this characteristic which had apparently been so happily discovered might go towards throwing some light on the origins of an idea of an earlier group of thinkers, an idea, incidentally, originating in much the same way as the aforementioned linguistic theory.

Briefly, the thing might be styled 'The Anti-holiday'. Its theoretical basis is as follows. Holidays are supposed to be for resting, traditionally. Holidays are becoming increasingly unrestful, whether the form of unrest is that of driving long distances enclosed in a motor-car or of taking violent physical exercise ashore, afloat, underwater or in the air. The effect of such activity, nausea in the case of car driving, exhaustion in the case of violent exercise, could equally well be achieved without being put in the context of 'On holiday'. The participant could on the one hand obtain employment as a motorised 'Sales Representative', or on the other run up Arthur's Seat, jump into Bardowie Loch or improvise with the local equivalent. The point is that those who operate holidays have by some conjuring trick managed to persuade people that something which they would not dream of doing in their sober senses can, because it is done 'On holiday', become enjoyable. The effrontery of this is such that one might think that the tourist trade would feel justified in resting on its laurels for a millenium or two, but for the man of vision willing to take one more step there are glittering prizes (ie, money) to be had. Hence 'The Anti-holiday'.

To convey the essence of the idea it is necessary to give a few examples. First, there is the pony-trekking holiday. In the standard holiday of this sort, the guest is not only permitted to ride the pony but is also instructed in the rudiments of horse-management, which means being allowed to muck out the stable. In 'The Anti-holiday', the guest is not actually permitted to ride, but may use the beast for light ploughing, fetching down dead stags from inaccessible corries (not to be confused with the stalking anti-holiday, in which small groups of guests are dropped by helicopter on a lonely hillside and shot at by rich Italians, Spaniards and oil-men) and environmental recycling duties (dung-spreading). Or there is the anti-mystery tour, in which instead of embarking on a bus for an unknown destination sustained by a packed lunch provided by the operator, the guest remains in his home and a man arrives by van and takes away his lunch, the mystery being what he does with sixty rounds of Spam sandwiches, thirty oranges and four gallons of vacuum-flask tea. Or there is the anti-stately home holiday, in which impoverished members of the lesser aristocracy spend a week-end in your home, joining you in such typical pleasures as watching the Des O'Connor Show while enjoying a Roast Beef TeeVee Supper and a glass of pale ale. These are just a few possibilities which are offered with due humility to the Scottish Tourist Board for consideration. After all, everyone needs a holiday.

July 1975

Highland Village

In the heart of the Highlands, nestling at the foot of Ben Esserie, you will find the village of Gloaming. It consists of twenty or so little grey cottages, a village hall and a post office which is still selling World Cup T-shirts. Half a mile up the road is a caravan site owned by a man who left Birmingham to get away from it all and now caters for two hundred caravanners by providing space, a camp shop stocking everything from Mary Stewart to deep-frozen chilli con carne, and a short-order restaurant equipped with a juke-box and a pool table. The locals avoid the shop, preferring to buy their provisions from an old-time van which comes up the glen once a week. Occasionally they drive off to the nearest big town and return in cars cluttered with wire-netting, gumboots and tins of cat food. In the village hall whist-drives are held on Tuesdays. The Film Society which used to meet there closed at about the same time as the craft shop.

The local hotel, the Macomnium Arms, caters mostly for fishermen. It is a complicated Victorian building, abruptly dotted with new fire doors and hung with stuffed trout taken long summers ago from the waters of nearby Loch Chuddie. The fishermen spend the evenings full of indifferent dinner, working their way through an impressive range of malt whiskies but failing to glean any useful tips from the bar person, a transitory Australian called Shirlene. In the public bar, where notices of long-gone social evenings hang by the door and the dart-board looks like a well-nibbled chocolate biscuit, a slow old man pours pints for slow old men to drink. The caravanners stay away. For a time, profits were swollen by the rum-drinking navvies who built the new, less picturesque road up the side of Loch Chuddie. On the night before the final section was to be declared open by minor royalty, the foreman drank a rum or two extra and painted on the ground opposite the official dias the words 'Macmenemy's Motorway'. The proprietor of the hotel, a businessman from Lanarkshire, does not like the locals and each New Year closes for redecoration. The nearest pint is then twelve miles away, over the hill at Rhodie.

Occasionally the bar is brightened with the orange and scarlet of hillwalkers attracted by the prospect of the celebrated and far from easy ascent of Ben Esserie. Their equipment litters the floor and they drink little, but the proprietor thinks that they add some sort of authenticity and encourages them. One summer he arranged a mini-folk festival, featuring the Smokey Mountain Boys from Musselburgh. The hillwalkers stayed away.

Passing tourists are now encouraged to stop by the local authority's Littermore picnic area and the Mendacious nature trail. The former is a square of earth beneath some weedy alders on the shores of Loch Chuddie. Tables and chairs hewn from fallen trees vie for space with litter-bins and ticket-machines. Chaffinches swoop on fragments of vinegar chipy. Near by the nature trail goes steeply up through stands of Sitka spruce, across a bog, out onto the moor and back. The guidebook combines robust good sense about land use and contrasting soil structures with coy hints about sighting pine-martens, roe deer and wild cat. It is illustrated with drawings of fir cones and otters' tracks. The gullible accept it; the gullible ignorant look hopefully skyward, believing the pine-marten to be a bird.

The big house at the head of the loch is for sale again. It was bought from the last of the Macomniums by a lace millionaire from Nottingham, who put his keepers and ghillies into a personal tweed of his own devising and slaughtered grouse and salmon at an astonishing rate in the company of the cream of Edwardian society. His great-grandson, the present owner, is studying maritime ecology in Florida and has never set eyes on Gloaming.

May 1980

Scots Worthies

It is not for us to advise our contemporaries, but it is arguable that *The Scots Law Times* lost something, all those years ago, when it dropped its illustrated pocket biographies of leading members of the profession. We do not know how many hands were behind those lapidary paragraphs, but certainly a nice house style was developed, especially for dealing with the less dramatic aspects of the life of each subject. Take this, for example: 'Mr Thomson is a man of very few hobbies. He is no athlete, although he bicycles.' A kinder reference to another solicitor goes as follows: 'His time for the mile was wonderful, considering the track on which he had to run.'

Naturally, the author occasionally repeats himself; in particular, when inspiration flags, he is inclined to seek refuge in some such phrase as: 'While his diligence rapidly acquired him an extensive practice, his genial nature won him the high esteem of a large number of friends.'

None the less, a glimpse into these pages, especially the ones which cover the years leading up to the Great War, is entertaining and instructive. We are in a world of solidarity, a world where a man is judged on his professional ability, his public service and the quality of his friendships. Principal recreations, which are almost always referred to, are golf and shooting, although motoring makes a somewhat scandalous appearance. One advocate is referred to as being 'a chauffeur qualified to undertake roadside repairs'. And it is said of a Writer to the

Signet: 'In pre-motor days he was a first-rate long-distance walker, doing with ease 100 miles at a stretch, over rough country.' The eclipse of the bicycle is regretted—and no wonder. Of one KC we are told: 'In his leisure hours he combines a devotion to the bicycle with the culture of theology.' while of a Keeper of the Register of Deeds, we hear: 'He also rode on a tricycle—an art which he acquired after he had reached his sixty-fifth year.'

The subjects of these tributes range from Senators down. One nice touch is a description of a judge in that he 'had a dislike, almost amounting to intolerance, of all irrelevance and waste of time, and that sometimes brought him into conflict with one or two of the procurators in his court'. One wonders if he ever had to listen to the advocate of whom it was written: 'His judgment was sound rather than rapid.' Certainly he sounds the sort of person who would justify the attitude brought out in this rather nice tribute to a Writer to the Signet: 'He was rarely seen in Parliament House because he did his best to keep his clients out of it.' And what would he have made of the advocate of whom the apologist says: 'Though his views on many subjects were worthy of notice, he somehow failed to express himself adequately by word of mouth'?

Generally speaking, these short biographies deal with the better side of their subjects' natures. Of an advocate it is remarked: 'As a social entertainer of chosen friends, Mr B is perhaps without a rival.' But what is one to make of the following remark? Is there a hidden dig? 'The Sheriff Court of Aberdeen is fortunate in having a more than respectable tradition. . . .'

Of all these worthies, who is the most worthy? Two perhaps spring to mind. The first is the KC who 'despised digests, and used to boast that he could put his hand on any volume of the reports which contained the case he wanted after not more than three tries'. Of this gentleman it was also written: 'His questions were like blows of a cudgel, delivered with great rapidity and unerring dexterity.' But pride of place must surely go to him of whom it is recorded: 'At least one Glasgow lawyer can quote Homer by the book and construe a Greek chorus with any Oxford Don.' Any takers?

March 1980

Playing the Game

'Rain stops Scottish cricket' said the headline with an air of terse familiarity, reminding one again of that determination bordering on folly which leads people to practise in one kind of surroundings a sport or pastime designed for quite different conditions.

Cricket, English-style, is a splendid game. A chance meeting with a man in a public house in deepest Kent led to my involvement that afternoon on the village green, where the sun shone from noon till night, someone on each side scored a century and a horse stood on the ball to the consternation of the timorous city-dweller sent to fetch it. It was a delightful afternoon, enjoyed by all, even the stockbroker who fielded in dark glasses, spoke to no one and topped himself up during the frequent unscheduled interruptions in play by easing across to the boundary where his recumbent wife would hand him a glass filled from a dangerous-looking aluminium cocktail shaker.

Cricket in Scotland, on the contrary, is a damp depressing game, filled with memories of staring in a melancholy way at framed team photos, slightly foxed, while the rain comes down like stair-rods and everyone tries to agree that the sky is starting to look brighter. The point, presumably, is that it is enough for the true addict to stand there padded up to the eyeballs and waving his bat in a series of wristy cuts at the stale air of the dressing-room, fulfilled through a vigorous exercise of the imagination to an extent that an actual innings could only diminish.

In order that the imagination should be able so to work, it seems necessary that the paraphernalia of the actual should be present. While hitching in France and looking for a place to spend the night, I met a spelaeologist who, living far from limestone country, had of necessity built his own pothole, complete with stalagmites and stalactites, in the back garden. He permitted me to spend the night there and it was quite revolting, since his passion for detail had driven him to include a sensible modicum of underground dampness and an open chimney up which the wind soughed and whistled with a lugubrious persistence which banished sleep. In a way, though, this sort of excess, this insistence that for the purpose of pursuing one's chosen sport that which would not otherwise be there shall be there, is not so different from foxhunters who take the precaution of letting the occasional fox out of a box, or fishermen who fill up the loch with young trout from the fish-farm. No doubt both would prefer the genuine article but are willing to compromise to an extent.

The danger about the foregoing is that all sports are dependent on the rules which define them, so that if you alter them too much you end up with a different sport. One example of this is fly-fishing, a subject on which I express myself with that assurance which comes from almost complete ignorance. To fish with a dry fly involves, as well as a deal of physical dexterity, an ability to make computer-like calculations based on wind, water, light and temperature in order to arrive at the right fly. While all this is being done, as like as not in a light breeze which threatens to put the hook into the back of the beginner's neck at every cast, there are enormous succulent trout swimming voraciously below. Is it any wonder that the hapless worm should occasionally come to hand, or rather to hook? But by that simple gesture one is out of the classy world of the fly-fisher and into the realm of the wee boy with the bent pin. What are they going to say, when easily rehearsing the magical names of famous flies, if you chip in with the information that you took two nice whiting with an old curtain rod and a bit of rancid pork?

I suppose the happiest sportsmen are those who make their own rules and usually stick to them, sometimes awarding themselves a putt which they did not quite hole, or taking another throw with the dart which bounced out of the board. That is my opinion. I leave you to ponder that of R. S. Surtees, the hunting writer: 'No man is fit to be called a sportsman wot doesn't kick his wife out of bed on a haverage once in three weeks!'

August 1973

The Dog Bus Leaves at 5 am

Recently we have had the pleasure of reading about the adventures of people who bought islands, became vets in the thirties, founded seal sanctuaries, ate their friends after Andean plane crashes and fell off mountains. It was with a skip of joy and a grunt of relief that we curled up on the sofa with a box of Turkish delight and Miss Hagbury Dick's latest opus, for here, surely, we would find again that civilised elegance and human warmth that marks everything Miss Hagbury does. Or almost. How rude was our awakening! for in this latest work our author has forsaken her equally familiar worlds of the hospital ward and the '45 rebellion, calm, colourful and comforting as they are, for the social realism and rural squalor of the world of the professional dog-breeder and his victims, canine and human.

Consider this beginning: 'I woke up. My mouth felt like a puppies' pissoir. Somewhere behind my temples the Barking Dogs were giving out with "Jingle Bells" in the key of F-sharp. Painfully I tried to put together the events of the night before. A hard game of squash with Abdulla Khan, the wily old professional at the Royal Caledonian Rackets Club. A well-fought session at the backgammon board where I took the Regius Professor of Astronomy for a fistful of Krugerrand. A few pints of champagne with some kindred spirits, culminating in an animated discussion with a swarthy stranger wearing the ribbon of the *médaille d'honneur* of the Kennel Club in the lapel of his immaculate Savile Row suit. And then. . . . A mournful howling from across the room jerked me into wakefulness. There staring at me across the room was the largest, most evil Pomeranian wolf-hound I had ever seen. And he looked like he wanted his breakfast.' A different sort of opening from the author's *Tell to Me, Troubadour*: 'Morag shyly averted her eyes. "I'm afraid this waltz is taken, Lord Alastair," she whispered.'

Further research reveals that her hero, Dirk Sprague, witty, resourceful and with an endearing twist to his thick right eyebrow, has indeed been sold a pup. A visit to the family solicitors, Joblot & Jerrybuilt, reveals that the nest of papers amid which the canine guest has passed the night is a deed of sale for Stranraer Mulberry III, a pooch with a better pedigree than the Duke of Edinburgh and every chance of taking top honours at the forthcoming Commonwealth Dog Show, Meadowbank. The eagle eye of senior partner Jocelyn Joblot observes that it is a condition of the contract that the new owner exhibits the beast at the show, and his remark 'If you fall down on this one it's Carey Street for you. They've got conditions in here that would make a Trappist Monk commit a breach of the peace', if perhaps unlikely to be uttered by a President of the Law Society, certainly gets the point across.

Dirk, however, is made of stronger stuff. Nonchalantly observing that when his foot is on his native heath there's not a writ-server that could get within a million miles of him among the corries of Bennachie (Miss Dick here seems to be harking back to the subject-matter of her earlier successes), he ships the hound aboard his four-masted schooner *Potemkin* lying off Granton, and sets sail from the effete south for the port of Peterhead and freedom.

Things do not go smoothly for our hero. Putting into Arbroath for hardtack and fresh water, the Dutch mate negligently allows the dog to slip overboard. Eventually it is recaptured with its head in a barrel of smokies, but not before Dirk has been fined the maximum by a sheriff whose natural distaste for livestock has been wildly aggravated by a *Panorama* programme on rabies. This swingeing blow to the family fortunes leaves Dick tottering on the verge of penury. We next find him sitting in the baronial hall of his ancestral home, a glass of Glen Moray 93 (Daiches on Whisky, p 155: 'Of tremendous stature, yet full of grace') clutched in the sunburnt fingers of his elegant hand. He is musing as he looks around him. 'The sporran which Leofric Sprague picked up after the Battle of Largs, the contents of

The Dog Bus Leaves at 5 am

which helped found the family fortunes. The half-consumed boiled egg which the Young Pretender left, abruptly, to resume his flight among the heather. The chair which Arthur Negus sat on during a charity performance of *Going for a Song*. All these priceless relics of a great family, all these would have to go unless. . . .' The night draws on towards dawn. Dirk, his brain in a fever, conceives the mad, reckless plan of dashing south with the dog, to win the prize, to pay the fine and to avoid the appalling consequences of his breach of contract. But he has no money for the fare. Unbeknown to him, however, but fortunately known to his sole remaining retainer, Glenbucket, impoverished dog-owners from Wick to the Howe of the Mearns have clubbed together to hire a charabanc which even now is wending its way south, stopping to pick up its cargo at croft and hamlet. It is at this point that Miss Dick leaves us hanging in suspense and dying for the sequel, as Glenbucket leans across and whispers in his master's ear, 'Sir, the dog-bus leaves at five am.'

July 1976

Some overheard remarks

Kelvinbridge, Glasgow
Fat young trendy, staggering out of pub on the way to his Alfa late at night, to tinker woman with five weans: 'Are you letting these children beg for you? That's the most disgusting thing I've ever seen!' (Is sick round corner, overcome by it all.)

Musselburgh talent competition
'And a big hand for Gary who's walked all the way from Danderhall to be with us tonight.' (Sings 'My Way' all the way back.)

Biggar pottery exhibition
'Very nice, very clever. Just another thing to dust, though!' (Thus spake Araldite, Goddess of Ceramics.)

October 1987

A Lacuna in the Palimpsest

Flann O'Brien, 'the best comic writer I can think of', according to S. J. Perelman (who is the best comic writer I can think of), is the pseudonym of a Dublin journalist, Brian O'Nolan, who died in 1966. Just to confuse matters, he used the *nom de plume* Myles na Gopaleen for his column in the *Irish Times*, which in turn was named, charmingly, 'Cruiskeen Lawn', which translates as the 'Full Little Jug'. What na Gopaleen means I do not know, but would like to. If you are beginning to lose the drift, that's fine, for that is the sort of effect the man has.

I never met him, but I did know an Irish doctor called Rory O'Moore, whose wife, a Norwegian, had seen him drunk on a bus in Dublin. James Joyce, who did know him, called him a real writer with the true comic spirit. Flann O'Brien retaliated to this praise, which was directed towards his novel *At Swim-Two-Birds*, by making Joyce a character in *The Dalkey Archive*, which came out in 1964. According to this account, the author of *Ulysses* is discovered, long after he is supposed to be dead, living near Dublin and trying to persuade the Jesuits that he has a Late Vocation to join. He reveals that the great book was not written by him at all, though his name was used, but by 'Muckrakers, obscene poets, carnal pimps, sodomous sycophants, pedlars of the coloured lusts of fallen humanity. Please don't ask me for names'. This revelation comes at the end of a book hitherto dominated by the belief of one Police Sergeant Fottrell that because of something called 'The Mollycule Theory', his friend

Michael Gilhanney has become part person, part bicycle, as a result of riding over the rocky roadsteads of the parish for too many years, causing the interchanging of mollycules between them.

Some of the themes and jokes of this book are continued in *The Third Policeman*, but there is a darker, more serious air to that book, perhaps because the author had found a way of using comedy for tragic purposes. The first sentence, which contains a curious echo of the assault by the Playboy of the Western World on his father, sets the tone of the book: 'Not everybody knows how I killed old Phillip Mathers, smashing his jaw in with my spade; but first it is better to speak of my friendship with John Divney because it was he who first knocked old Mathers down by giving him a great blow in the neck with a special bicycle-pump which he had manufactured himself out of a hollow iron bar.' This blend of the matter-of-fact and the grotesque is characteristic.

In spite of the considerable comic virtuosity of *The Hard Life*, which deals with two orphan brothers growing up in the home of the mysteriously humanitarian Mr Collopy, the elder of them preparing for the rigours to come by teaching people by post how to walk the tightrope and subsequently inventing the 'London University Academy', Flann O'Brien's masterpiece is usually considered to be *At Swim-Two-Birds*. I remember coming upon it in a newsagent's shop in St Andrews one wet day some fifteen years ago and being struck by the inventive Celtic-style jacket and impressive encomiums of praise by the likes of Graham Greene and Dylan Thomas in which the publishers had dressed it. I was even more struck by what was inside. Briefly, it is a novel about a youth writing a novel about a novelist whose characters revolt against his treatment of them and get their own back by writing about him while he is asleep. It's a wild blend of parody, fantasy, wit and low comedy. Sweeny, the mad King of Ireland, crashes and collides with invisible leprechauns, drunken students, Dublin cattle-rustlers, Victorian villains, and so on and so on. It is wildly inventive and very addictive.

I mentioned earlier the activities of O'Brien as na Gopaleen and I'm happy to say that a collection of these pieces is currently available, published by Picador under the title of *The Best of Myles*. The level of comic invention here is quite extraordinary. As with Beachcomber, na Gopaleen liked to invent characters and to trot them out again and again for the edification of his readers. Here we have 'The Plain People of Ireland', a character not unlike Beachcomber's Prodnose, slow to see the joke and suspicious of being imposed upon; 'The Brother', who never appears but whose astounding intellectual achievements are recounted by his admiring sibling; and perhaps best of all, the punning poets, Keats and Chapman. Their discussion, for instance, of the problem of whether the prophets of dialectical materialism should have recommended scientific breeding of humans in the way which has been so successful with racehorses, ends with the melancholy reflection that foals rush in where Engels fears to tread.

February 1977

P.S. (1988) I am told na Gopaleen means 'of the little horses'. But why?

Received ideas

Pipistrelle
A diminutive French chanteuse who protected her non-Aryan lover from the Germans by keeping him in her golf-bag with a woolly cap on his head. When the story came out after the war, Pépé-le-Niblick, as his friends called him, was so mortified that he refused to go on treating her badly.

Cabbage White
Southern area light-heavyweight champion who fought a courageous draw with Freddie Mills before going on to end his days in the W. Barrington Dalby Institute for the Hopelessly Bewildered.

Chanterelle
This popular vocalist fell from favour in the *boîtes-de-nuit* of Aberdeen when the *Sunday Post* revealed that she was not, after all, a transsexual from Toulon. 'Chanterelle—Chanty Wrassler—its Effie Duff frae Pitmedden!' was the headline.

June 1986

Bizarre Bazaar

Browsing through the small ads in *The Sunday Times* recently, I came across this: 'Pyramid Energy—Try it yourself—it's amazing!' Unfortunately the author of the text did not go on to give details of what might be expected from this phenomenon, and in particular did not say whether the energy involved could be applied to the human frame. It sounded just the thing, though, if for the stated £10.95 one could crawl under the steel shape and, through some freak of atmospheric concentration, utilise the forces of the universe to help with filling in a VAT return or deciding on the cheapest way to reach the Argentine. Lyall Watson in *Supernature* goes on a bit about pyramids and their miraculous powers, instancing the fact that a razor blade placed at the centre of the structure will retain its sharpness despite use. This sounds a bit like that other thing which keeps cropping up in the small ads, the three-in-one plastic utensil with which you can trim the family's hair and save £££s. Somehow the smallness of the copy and the extravagance of the promised benefits go well together. Where the 'Very Godzilla-very Sandersons' have a slack-bellied softness about them, the little fellows are real fighters. It does seem a bit much, though, when Collins take a small space to boost the sales of their well-known bestseller, the Bible, hiring Roy Castle to put in a Good Word for the Good Book. Next thing we'll have the Pope recommending the best buy in trumpets and dancing pumps.

In the breast of the *Sunday Telegraph* reader, if the ads are anything to go by, there is a troubled spirit, a daemon at odds with itself. What is he thinking of, this person, as he whiles away the Sabbath, his city suit exchanged for a submariner's poloneck, just the thing to wear while clearing the blocked drains with a gadget so hot off the drawing board that they have not even had time to give it a name, round his wrist a Rumaton bracelet with built-in magnets, and round his waist a nylon wallet belt in which his money, jewellery and documents are kept safe from thieves, pickpockets and muggers? Surely he dreams of his wife, even now out in the African-hardwood-befloored kitchen, dispensing with expensive teabags and messy teapots by skilfully brewing a cuppa in a specially hinged, perforated spoon while removing hard skin and callouses with the sensational German Foot Parer. Not thus does he see her, though. In his mind's eye she reclines on a pine bed by Moriarti, her Banner dress, such incredible value for the fuller figure, cast carelessly aside; under the Union Jack bedspread, back by popular demand, wearing no more than an item of exotic corsetry of the sort she'd never dared wear before. Maddened with conjugal lust, he quite forgets to close the super-quality Venetian blinds in his haste to tear off his exclusive orange Swim-Kinis, while the friendly neighbourhood peeping Tom adjusts the focus to a sharp close-view and reflects that these Power-X binoculars really are fantastic value at £6.50.

April 1978

The Strange Case of Deacon Brodie

Scottish writers have often found pleasure in toying with the idea of the double life. James Hogg, in the *Justified Sinner*, used the notion to create a masterpiece of psychological fiction. R. L. Stevenson, in *The Strange Case of Dr Jekyll and Mr Hyde*, gave a new expression to the language, although when one turns to the book itself it becomes clear that common usage has altered the original meaning. In a recently published book which will fascinate anyone interested in the literature and the law of Scotland, John S. Gibson has examined that story and attempted to identify its origins. His title, *Deacon Brodie: Father to Jekyll and Hyde*, speaks for itself. I must say at the outset that I wish it were longer, so many ideas does Mr Gibson throw off, but perhaps he will return to these themes.

Briefly, the scheme is as follows. The criminal career and trial of Deacon Brodie are set out in a concise and evocative way. The problem which faces any student of Brodie is why he embarked on a course of conduct which was bound to lead to his disgrace and death. Again, popular usage gets it wrong, for with Brodie we are not dealing with a man respectable by day and villainous by night. By the time of his flight after the botched attempt at breaking into the Excise Office, Brodie was widely known as a man who enjoyed bad company. Mr Gibson lays considerable emphasis on the performances of West Digges as Macheath, the dashing highwayman, in *The Beggar's Opera*, then in frequent performance at the new Theatre Royal, as making Brodie something more than 'another card in the Edinburgh pack'.

The trial presents us with a different problem, and it is here that Mr Gibson really excels, particularly in his excavation of the political motives of the judges and counsel involved.

In order that Brodie and his co-accused George Smith could be prosecuted successfully, it was necessary that the Crown should be able to adduce the evidence of one John Brown, formerly an accomplice. Brown had been convicted of theft and sentenced to transportation at the Middlesex Sessions some time before. He was a fugitive from this sentence and normally he would have been incompetent as a witness. What the prosecution argued with success was that the exercise of the royal prerogative of pardon, which had been extended to Brown, was effective to override the fact that by the law of Scotland he was debarred. It was to this point that the Whig lawyers for the defence addressed themselves; this is the reason for the tenacious (and incorrect) insistence of John Clerk, Smith's counsel, that the jury were the judges of the law as well as of the facts. In other words, he and the Dean of Faculty, Henry Erskine, argued the constitutional question in their different ways, right to the end of the trial. One cannot help feeling that to some extent their motives had more regard for general political questions than for the welfare of their clients, but they were probably beyond defending. On the other hand, it appears from Mr Gibson's account that the Crown was now at its own dubious game, for a few months before in the same court there had been a murder trial in which the same John Brown should clearly have been a co-accused, and much of what was said about the effect of the royal pardon is thus exposed as humbug. Accordingly, while agreeing with the suggestion made by Lord Cameron in his incisive foreword that Braxfield, the presiding judge, has been misrepresented (and that by RLS too, in *Weir of Hermiston*) and that he deserves a volume to himself as lawyer, judge and man of his century, this aspect of the case should not be forgotten. Nor should the fact that on the jury was one of Brodie's old acquaintances, William Creech, the bookseller, whose account of the trial was out within the week.

As if there was not enough to stir the imagination in what Mr Gibson has already told us, he then takes up the theme which is predicated in his title. There has been so much sentimental claptrap committed to print about Stevenson by his hagiographers, especially those who like to think of him as the perennial sickly child waiting for the lamplighter to come by, that it is something of a shock to discover that in fact he described the town of his youth as 'a vicious, lamp-lit fairyland'. It is more than likely that the youthful Stevenson was at one time in love with a prostitute from one of the establishments at the east end of the New Town. Mr Gibson identifies the area—nominally in London, where *Jekyll and Hyde* is set—with the now demolished St James's Square. In a most persuasive passage he suggests that Stevenson's play *Deacon Brodie or The Double Life* failed because the motives there given to Brodie, avarice and addiction to gambling, were afflictions unknown to the author, whereas when he returned to the theme in *Jekyll and Hyde*, 'the kind of double life he described was rooted in an area of experience and observation of which the younger Stevenson had searing memories'.

My admiration for Mr Gibson's work in this book is enormous. It is a genuine achievement of critical imagination. He deserves our gratitude, and so does his publisher.

July 1977

Who wrote, and where:
(*a*) 'If the law supposes that,' said Mr Bumble . . . 'the law is a ass. . . .'
(*b*) Laws are like cobwebs, which may catch small flies, but let wasps and hornets back through.
(*c*) Mrs Bertram: 'That sounds like nonsense, my dear.'
Mr Bertram: 'May be so, my dear; but it may be very good law for all that.'
(*d*) He saw a Lawyer killing a viper
On a dunghill hard by his own stable;
And the Devil smiled, for it put him in mind
Of Cain and his brother, Abel.
(*e*) . . . I mete and dole
Unequal laws unto a savage race.

Answers
(*a*) Charles Dickens, *Oliver Twist*; (*b*) Jonathan Swift, *A Tritical Essay*; (*c*) Sir Walter Scott, *Guy Mannering*; (*d*) Samuel Taylor Coleridge, *The Devil's Thoughts*; (*e*) Lord Tennyson, *Ulysses*.

December 1981

Boundless, Endless and Subminimal

There came through the post not long ago a card bearing a design of blue and pink jagged stripes, with a terse sentence underneath about the fact that during the First World War a lot of ships were sunk by submarines which disliked modern art. The shape, the ships, the cool confidence of the statement, all this was unmistakable. So it was that an early evening a few nights later found me expectant outside the Scottish Arts Council Gallery, intent on seeing an exhibition of recent work by Ian Hamilton Finlay.

Mr Finlay began, I think, as a poet. Certainly he achieved his first fame with a book of deceptively small poems called *The Dancers Inherit the Party*, published by his own Wild Hawthorn Press. This was followed by a jokey little collection of epigrams in the patois, called *Glasgow Beasts and a Burd*, subtitled 'A wee buik for big weans', which came out in 1961 and gave a lot of pleasure. About the same time I remember enjoying a dramatic piece, *Walking Through Seaweed*, at the Festival Fringe. Mr Finlay is also a short-story writer, with, for example, two pieces in J. F. Hendry's *Penguin Book of Scottish Stories*.

During the sixties, however, his interest seemed to turn in the direction of what was called concrete poetry. This art form was never particularly popular in Great Britain and from then on Mr Finlay has probably enjoyed a higher reputation in Europe and the USA than at home. His controversial poems are not easy to come by. In the *Penguin Book of Scottish Verse* he is not represented, an omission which is curious but, considering the effect that Mr Finlay and the Scottish literary scene have on one another, perhaps not surprising. He does have a poem, a characteristic blend of gentleness and astringency, 'Black Tomintoul', in Antonia Fraser's *Scottish Love Poems*. Concrete poetry is much concerned with the position of the word on the page as an integral part of the poem. From this, Mr Finlay's work has come more and more to be in the form of picture or sculpture. In particular, he has developed a passion for carved stones. One such I saw not long ago in the Botanical Gardens, polished and carved, and I recall, with the words 'Bring back the birch'. This may be an apposite piece of art in its environment or it may be rather predictable whimsy. While the experimentation with ponds and stones and ships and sundials continued, the Fulcrum Press planned a collection of Mr Finlay's earlier poems. Whether or not this ever really came out I do not know. I do remember a furious, long-lasting and far-reaching row in which Mr Finlay sought redress from his publishers for their describing the book, also entitled *The Dancers Inherit the Party*, as a first edition, while berating the Scottish Arts Council for dragging its feet instead of racing to his support.

A mutual friend involved me briefly with Mr Finlay over this, although I fear that my advice neither pleased nor helped him. His last communication was a post-card which carried on one side a red elbow-like shape, 'The sign of the nudge', and on the other the sentence 'Are we to interpret your silence as a thoughtful one?'

Coming up to date, however, I must report that along with another two hundred or so people I failed to see the exhibition that evening. Instead, a depressed man with his collar turned up against the world's rough winds sent us away, saying that the artist had telephoned minutes before the opening to withdraw his pictures. What a happening! Was this the ultimate in minimalist art, the farthest a conceptionalist would go, a whole gallery full of artefacts which no one was allowed to see, while, outside, Charlotte Square swarmed with shuffling aesthetes? What symbolism, that all that kept the watchers from the watched should be the fabric of the Arts Council building! No such luck. Apparently Mr Finlay had had another row, this time with the English weekly *The Spectator*. They had behaved ungraciously towards him and again the SAC had failed when its support was most needed. It seemed a pity, altogether. Even the invitation has been thrown out now, accidentally, so all that remains of the show, for me, is the foregoing. Most confusing.

July 1978

Pick-pockets of Literature

I thought this month that I would write a piece on the extent to which Eastern bloc countries' advertising of cheap watches, radios, etc, in the columns of down-market British newspapers was beginning to pay off in terms of increasing orders. I thought that I would do so not because of any inside information I might have, but because it would permit the Production Editor of the *Journal*, who supplies Petronius with his monthly title, to commit something on the lines of 'Red Sales in "The Sun" Set'. If you don't think much of that, read no further.

The pun is probably the humorous device over which people divide most sharply. It is also a device which can be feeble in the extreme or enormously effective. An example of the feeble end of the scale, I suppose, might be found in those little headlines which newspapers slip in over filler paragraphs of inconsequential news. You know the sort of thing: 'A man stuck on Ben Nevis successfully attracted the attention of rescue parties by setting fire to his trousers and swinging them round his head', to which the caption is 'Heat Wave?' At a more elevated level, an interesting, if somewhat technical, examination of the pun in literature is to be found in William Empson's *The Seven Types of Ambiguity*. Shakespeare, for example, was very fond of a pun, as were many writers working at a time when language was relatively new and charged with meaning. To an extent, the joy of a pun is in the way in which it strikes together opposites to produce a flash of either heat or light. Much Shakespearian comedy is virtually incomprehensible to us nowadays because it depends on puns which we do not understand, and the Sonnets, which were presumably written for a small, highly educated readership, also make considerable use of the pun. The most unremitting punster among the English poets, however, must have been Thomas Hood, responsible for such lines as:

'His death, which happen'd in his berth,
At forty-odd befell:
They went and told the sexton, and
The sexton toll'd the bell.'

Hood used the pun to make jokes; subsequent practitioners like James Joyce and Dylan Thomas have used it more seriously, in an attempt to try to convey or suggest more than one meaning through a single word. One's feeling here, however, is that unlike the Elizabethans' use of the pun, when language was fresh and the very discovery of a pun an instance of its vitality, twentieth-century writers have been driven to deliberate ambiguity in an effort to restore some strength to our jaded and slack speech. In *Ulysses*, for example, Joyce has a rather complicated pun which runs throughout the book, based on an advertising slogan which Leopold Bloom sees as he wanders about Dublin: 'What is home without Plumrose's Potted Meat? Incomplete. With it, an abode of bliss.' To begin to understand what this is all about, one has to appreciate that the chief reason for, or symptom of, the unhappiness which exists between Bloom and his wife Molly is that it is a number of years since they last had sexual relations. The pun, then, is built up as follows. There is a similarity in sound, if one uses a Dublin accent, between the words 'Bloom' and 'Plum'. We know from the soliloquy that Molly, who comes from Gibraltar, associates the rose with sexual experience. 'Potted meat' was, and for all I know may still be, a fairly obvious synonym for sexual intercourse. That is the basis of the pun. But it is part of Joyce's style to allude constantly to it throughout the book—for example, in a very funny passage about two old ladies who have climbed the obviously phallic Nelson's Monument and are eating plums and dropping the stones off the top.

Part of the difficulty often associated with reading Joyce is that of keeping alert to his allusions. A pun missed is a pun pointless, although perhaps it works away at a subconscious level. One pun which I have noticed only since beginning this piece occurs towards the end of Kingsley Amis's clever poem 'A Song of Experience'. The poem tells of some people having a drink who invite a commercial traveller to tell them 'of women he had known'. He does so, and the poem concludes with his leaving.

'I saw him, brisk in May, in Juliet's weather,
Hitch up the trousers of his long-tailed suit,
Polish his windscreen with a chamois-leather,
And stow his case of samples in the boot.'

For a long time I thought this no more than a neat vignette, but I wonder now. Is there a connection between a long tale and a tall story? Is a person who wears a long-tailed suit a long-tailed (or taled) suitor? There might not be a pun here, but then again there might.

October 1975

Skiing done badly is the saddest of all sports, man out of his element, ungainly and undignified. Animals, who are sensible about such things, hibernate when the snow comes down. Incredibly, men who in other aspects of their lives are manifestly successful, rich and kind, with attractive wives and intelligent children, feel driven to trudge through blizzards to emulate the achievements of men who are younger, fitter and stupider. No one in their senses would ski if they could avoid it. If skiing were a necessity, then such men would pay other people to do it for them. By being an unnecessary inconvenience, it becomes a luxury. They say it is nice afterwards, but so is sliding down the banisters into a tub of ice-water, and anyway the pleasures of *après-ski* amount to little more than the poor pupil buying countless drinks for his oafish instructor in an attempt, mysteriously, to re-establish some sort of social equilibrium. The depths of self-imposed degradation go not much lower.

December 1970

Artists' Visions

The National Gallery of Scotland has a fine new extension which burrows into the earth and at the moment is hanselling it with an exhibition illustrating the history of the Scottish landscape. This sets out to show through the work of various artists, mostly Scottish, how the landscape of Scotland came to be appreciated and represented. The Highlands of Scotland were discovered by Sir Walter Scott in the course of his invention of Loch Katrine and the Trossachs. While the hills had always been there, no one previously regarded them as much more than a nuisance, unfarmable, desolate and an obstacle to travel. Along came the Wizard of the North with his land of the mountain and the flood, my foot is on my native heath and so forth, and suddenly the Highlands were the thing. Earlier Robert Burns, a devout Lowlander, had felt compelled to make two Highland tours. The second extensive one seems to have been more successful than the first, on which the poet received some discourtesy at the hands of an innkeeper in Inveraray. He responded with the following lines:

'There's naething here but Highland pride,
And Highland scab and hunger;
If Providence has sent me here,
'Twas surely in an anger.'

On his next trip, Burns, in a happier frame of mind, wrote 'The Birks of Aberfeldy', visited the fiddler Neil Gow and was hospitably received by the Duke of Atholl. As a PR man, however, he was no Scott. Burns's tours, which he made in 1787, contrast remarkably with one in 1773, when James Boswell led Dr Johnson like a dancing bear through the glens and straths and out to the islands. Both enjoyed themselves, but their reaction to what they saw was scarcely rousing, much less romantic. Consider Johnson on the ruins of Inch Kenneth: 'It was not without some mournful emotion that we contemplated the ruins of religious structures, and the monuments of the dead.'

If it was Scott who presented the Highlands to the romantic imagination, he had an adept ally in the painter Sir Horatio McCulloch, some of whose mighty canvases are in the Edinburgh exhibition. Huge glowering mountains hang over stormy lochs, mist seeps up from the heather and disconsolate cattle sniff the sleety wind. Stern and wild indeed, but about the same time along came the great populariser, Landseer.

Sir Edwin Landseer, favourite painter of Queen Victoria, was an artist of staggering technical accomplishment. It is interesting that his name suggests that he was the Seer of the Landscape. Anyway, his picture of a red deer stag, 'Monarch of the Glen' (sold for 6,900 guineas in 1892), is still slaying them in Edinburgh.

'The stag at eve had drunk his fill,
Where danced the moon on Monan's rill,
And deep his midnight lair had made
In lone Glenartney's hazel shade'

was how Scott began his bestseller *The Lady of the Lake*. For myself, I've had my fill of Landseer's beast, noble horns, lachrymose eyes and velvet muzzle, but what can one say about a painting which has never lost the popularity it achieved when first exhibited in 1851? One answer is that it appeals to the lowest common denominator in popular taste. But at least its appeal is answered, unlike the new television programme *Scotch and Wry* which grovels in a paroxysm of self-abasement in its attempts to lick the public's hand. Fancy that once-good clown Rikki Fulton having to behave like one of Landseer's dogs.

After all, though, it's only a television programme, put out on Saturday nights in the slot which the BBC must believe to be watched only by those too drunk to turn off the set. As entertainment, the show is a non-starter, but as a twisted footnote to

Artists' Visions

the artists' visions of Scotland, as a reminder that the country has become an uglier place because people decided that it should be so, it has its place. Some of the old landscape men may have been no great shakes as painters, but their vision was one of optimism, not self-denigration.

November 1978

Where I go to rusticate, a small collection of houses somewhere between Melrose and Kelso, strange things are happening. The farmer's dog Sweep has just had nine puppies. They weren't intended, since she was really needed for her usual collie work, but it is lucky that they came since their father, the elderly and much-loved Snap, was accidentally lost not long after their conception. And, after thirty years in which there were no babies, in the last eighteen months there have been nappies drying outside five of the eleven houses. What's more, soon after a just-married couple moved into one of the cottages, they heard a mysterious knocking at the door one night and calls of 'Hello'—with no one there to be seen. A coming event casting its shadow before, perhaps?

My hope was that the knocking signified the return of the Brownie, although it is unlikely that he would draw attention to himself quite so blatantly. These little creatures, about three feet tall and stocky, with shaggy brown hair, used to be common around Border dwellings. They did a prodigious amount of work by night and the only reward expected was bread and milk, not put out for them, because that would suggest a sort of wage, but left where they could help themselves. They were notoriously sensitive to adverse criticism and also, perhaps surprisingly, to praise, which they seem to have felt implied dependence. Mostly they were reasonable enough if left alone to get on with things, although the one whose story is told by James Hogg in 'The Brownie of Black Haggs' seems vicious and vengeful, and the Brownie of Cranshaws, having overheard someone saying that he did not seem to have done the harvest so well this year, departed in a fury, throwing the crops over a cliff and vowing never to come back.

No one is sure who the Brownies really were. One attractive theory is that they were members of a previous race who hung around the homesteads of their successors, anxious to be of some use in return for a measure of food and protection but wary of too close a relationship, rather in the way that wild dogs must have been at once attracted and repelled by the campfires of our Neolithic forebears.

October 1987

Second Hand

That which is rare, say the economists, is not necessarily precious. This lesson used to be vividly illustrated by a professor in one of our universities who would hypothetically consider the value of a projected waistcoat made entirely out of fish scales. It is true, however, that if one is in search of a second-hand car, the object of one's choice becomes, so far as the motor trade is concerned, both rare and precious. Consider for example the following. There was on the market a car called the Morris 1000 Traveller. It was a car of proven merit, in that it did not fall to pieces when left out in the rain and was sufficiently large to accommodate as many children, parcels and dogs as any reasonable man could foresee the necessity of having to accommodate at one time. It enjoyed a steady sale and looked, we believe, like continuing to do so.

True, it had its drawbacks. The squarish build and wooden struts decorating the exterior were a far cry from the fastbacks and aerodynamic fins beloved of the more trendy Jehus de nos jours. The ambiance of the machine suggested not the ruthless suavity of a James Bond but the more traditional virtues of Ned Leithen and Archie Roylance. Nevertheless, it looked a good thing. Accordingly, its makers stopped making it. There was a brief silence while this fact was absorbed by the car-oriented public, which means not only the poor man's Fangios of Bridge of Weir and the Ingliston Light Infantry in their sheepskins and twills, but, sadly, all of us, even if our participation is limited to an old-fashioned avoidance of being knocked down. Thereafter advertisements began to appear extolling the virtues of this rare and much-sought-after vehicle; people selling began to feel that, in all decency, they had to insert a short explanation of their temerity in daring to dispose of this treasure, and would spend extra pennies on adding 'Owner going to New Zealand' or 'Beloved dog has outgrown back seat' or some such. One lady when I phoned to inquire about her advertisement was audibly reeling. 'I've been inundated,' she said.

I was bowling along the other day wondering how I was going to get my hands on one of these treasures when suddenly there it was, a lovely blue one doing a cautious twenty-five and packed to the gunnels with nuns, six or seven, and all in traditional kit. I got them in my sights and moved softly into the approach, but the sisters had obviously been accosted before. The one behind the wheel gunned it up to fifty and the chase was on. I followed them three times round the King's Theatre and across the Meadows and into Marchmont, where they lost me by going the wrong way up a one-way street and reversing through an automatic car-wash.

Like all good man-made laws of nature, the foregoing has its equal and opposite reaction, which is that if one is in the position of seller the car that but a year previously was a Koh-i-noor of its kind, is now squalidly common, universally execrated, an object of derision and contempt. To offer such an object for sale, those who condescend to blink an eye of interest imply, is about as fatuous as asking Sotheby's man round to value your garden gnome. Not only that, but beneath the steely eye of the dealer the tread miraculously erases itself from the tyres, rust blossoms like muscari, the bodywork dents and buckles and all projecting objects fall off. The powers of car salesmen are beyond those given to ordinary men. They are the spiritual successors of those horse-traders who covered the odd grey patch with boot polish in order to knock a dozen years off a nag or who, like Tommy Doem of the Pelican Livery Stables in Cripplegate, when asked about a horse replied that he had nothing in stock but a cow, 'but see her out at all events. Looking costs nothing'. Don't, whatever you do, look, is the moral, or you'll end up with a cow. And don't listen, either, or you'll end up believing that your shining chariot is no better than a dustbin on wheels and you should be grateful to the kind garage man for saving you the embarrassment of being seen about in it.

The reason for this funny situation is, I suppose, that unless we are constantly working with money we tend to regard it not as a commodity, but as a symbolic indicator of status or power. In the words of Robert Robinson, 'People blush and shuffle when money is at issue, like adolescents in a biology class.' It is this embarrassment which allows the car dealers of the world to work their wicked ways with us. Freed from sexual guilt, we still have a financial hang-up. Do not be ashamed of your wallet. It is natural and beautiful.

May 1972

Received ideas

Faculty of Advocates
Still attracts the country's top brains. They fight like dogs in court, then come out, shake hands and go for a cigarette and a glass of claret without even removing their wigs.

Albion Rovers
It is a shame that people won't support their local team, especially when it is a grand old one like this. 'There'll be dancing in the streets of Albion tonight!' 'Thank you, David.'

Avocado
A passing fad that came to stay.

John Logie Baird
All those lonely hours in the lab just so that we can watch Des O'Connor interviewing Bob Monkhouse. So much for the mission to explain.

Bannockburn
When shall we see their like again? Few people realise that Robert the Bruce was the same height as Princess Margaret.

'Slim' Jim Baxter
When you've said 'elegance', you've said it all. The pitch was his canvas (see Sobers, Gary).

The BBC
Too right wing by half. Subversive? I've heard worse from my Auntie Sheena after two sweet sherries and the Queen's Christmas Broadcast.

Lord Braxfield
He may have been a foul-mouthed curmudgeon, but he shaped our mercantile law. A giant among pigmies.

Certainties
Don't bet on them. The bookie always wins. It's a mug's game. The best site for a betting shop is between a Job Centre and a pub.

January 1987

Kay of Edinburgh

What do the following have in common? Dr Glen, who sought to buy his wife a second-hand coffin; Dr Joseph Black, discoverer of latent heat; Miss Burns, the beauty whom Edinburgh magistrates tried to banish for immorality; Francis Grosse, antiquary and object of Robert Burns's 'A chiel's amang you takin' notes/And, faith, he'll prent it'; Francis Jeffrey, Walter Scott and Adam Smith. The clue is in the last three, for they were all characters of Edinburgh's golden age, all had their likenesses done by the barber-turned-artist John Kay, and appear in a new edition of Hilary and Mary Evans's *John Kay of Edinburgh*.

Kay's work has always been regarded, with justification, as a valuable source of information for historians. Partly this is because his portraits were acknowledged in their time as faithful likenesses, partly because when a collection of his etchings was posthumously published in 1838, one James Paterson provided copious notes based on personal recollections of friends of the various subjects. The historical interest of the work has tended to overshadow the intrinsic merit of Kay's art and it was this state of affairs that the authors were concerned to remedy when the book first came out some seven years ago.

Kay was born near Dalkeith in 1742, was brought up (and ill-treated) by cousins in Leith, was apprenticed to a barber and eventually set up his own successful business in 1771. His talent as a draughtsman, as well as his engaging personality, brought him the patronage of one William Nisbet, and on the latter's death his heir settled on Kay an annuity of £20. Thereafter Kay was able to devote himself to his art, working from a shop in Parliament Close which became a popular resort for idlers eager to inspect the latest likenesses. Although his principal occupation was that of miniaturist, Kay was often of a satirical frame of mind, and that his lampoons could bite is evidenced by the fact that he was both persecuted and cudgelled by victims. He could be forthright with patrons too. One 'ill-looking man, much pimpled', who had commissioned a miniature for his fiancée, on complaining that the result was a poor likeness was told by Kay 'he would paint every plook in the puppy's face, would that please him?' Kay died at the age of eighty-four in 1826, leaving some nine hundred etchings.

The Evans's book is handsomely produced, with ninety-six full-page reproductions and a number of incidental illustrations, including a superbly composed self-portrait in oils and endpapers based on the great painting of Parliament House and Public Characters done in 1844 by a septemvirate which included Sir David Wilkie and Alexander Naysmith, which drew heavily on Kay's originals. Kay's work is characterised by a primitive and occasionally eccentric inventiveness. At times he is a caricaturist, as in his jibe at the self-made man who bought the big house at Falkirk then mistook the glare from the ironworks for the mob coming to burn him out. At other times, however, both by his clear facial details and his delineation of a subject's stance he is capable of considerable psychological penetration. A fine example of the latter Kay is 'The First Interview in 1786', which shows a bashful, rather simple burglar, George Smith, meeting the stylish and devious Deacon Brodie, whose bungling schemes were to bring them both to the scaffold. In their note, the authors say, 'The reason for the introduction of the dog and the cock is anyone's guess.' Mine is that, as appears from Forbes Bramble's excellent novel *The Strange Case of Deacon Brodie*, Smith's large dog involved itself in the preliminaries to the disastrous attempt to rob the Edinburgh Excise Office, and Brodie's passion was gambling on cockfights. Finally, it is worth mentioning a cunning little head of a grinning lawyer which, when turned upside down, becomes that of his anguished, grimacing client.

August 1980

Dirty Deeds 2

Mr Raymond Chandler Attends the Reading of the Will and Runs into Difficulties of Confidentiality

I stood out in the corridor on a length of carpet that was as deep as a baritone's boots trying to listen at a door that was as half-open as the Nixon administration. Inside, the legal eagle cleared his throat with a soft gurgle like a boiled egg bursting. Suddenly it was as quiet as a Scotch Sabbath.

'I will read the will,' he intoned.

Sitting in a high-backed chair that was as stuffed as a Spanish sausage, Julia Eckford, second wife of the deceased, sniffed back a tear that was as phoney as a fan-dancer's flattery. Against her widow's weeds her white face stood out like a snowman on a Hallowe'en cake. Tania Eckford stared at her stepmother with the calm loathing of a gardener with blowfly on his begonias.

The man of law added, 'But before I do so there is something which I should explain.'

As he spoke, somewhere behind me an equaliser gave a low popping sound like a pea-pod parting, and a slug creased my noggin. I went down like a dipsomaniac's deposit account.

Light came flooding back into my head like soda-water into a swimming-pool. I heard the legal eagle's tones, as dry and dusty as a Dead Sea donkey derby.

'. . . so you see, ladies, that really explains the whole thing. Tony didn't open the safe deposit until after Muller had purchased the reversionary rights, so that when Paccelli invited Lucille to the Gilded Parrot Club he can't have known about the DA's inquiries. If Mitzi had levelled with us in the first place, the Mexican bonds would still be. . . .'

They all began to smile at each other, like girl scouts at a gang-show. I edged forward as quietly as a mouse on mogadon, then my toe struck an abandoned deed-box with a bang like Big Ben blowing down. For a big man the attorney moved fast. His blackjack caught me on the right temple. As I vanished into a world that was as soft and black as a bad banana I heard his voice begin, 'First, to my beloved wife. . . .'

October 1979

Autumn is upon us, season of mists and mellow fruitfulness, if you are lucky enough to live somewhere soft like Kent, otherwise season of 'that wasn't much of a summer, was it?'—'the nights are drawing in' and 'oh dear me, here we are discussing the weather just like our perceptive neighbours in the European Community always say we do'. Perhaps the weather is the eternal topic, season in, season out, but other subjects do come and go with the turning year. We have just emerged from the months of holiday reminiscence, through the period of 'picked them up in the sales, twenty per cent off and you can scarcely notice the fire damage in the seat if you wear them outside in and sort of stoop at the right'. Before us stands 'well at least Auntie Lily is easy, two pounds of humbugs and a subscription to the *Scottish Field*' and 'no, as a matter of fact we were not invited, but I don't expect we would have been able to go anyway'.

November 1974

Landlord and Tenant

There died recently Eric Partridge, the lexicographer of slang, creator of a number of dictionaries of the vulgar which assist the scholar and delight the browser. If ever a man left his own monument it was he.

As it happens, the columnar 'we' has had occasion to make use of one of the chuckies from his cairn recently. With the aid of the *Smaller Slang Dictionary* we were able to translate the following poem, the manuscript of which was found stuffed into the toe of a wet wellington left behind in the minibus chartered by the Petronius Appreciation Society to take them on their annual outing to Maclay & Co's Thistle Brewery, Alloa.

Poem

I was sitting quiet at the Cain and Abel,
A gashion mug of gunfire in my hand,
When the Artful Dodger stuck his sticky beak in
And asked if I had had my baron band.

He's a dingbats dingo with a big bow window,
Very prone to come the acid and to rock,
But he knows that if he interrupts my grubstakes
I'll larrup him till he ends in dock.

So I told him kindly, 'Go and hump the bluey;
No buttinski's giving me the jim-jams, righty right.'
I reminded him he hadn't paid his Burton,
So he said he'd have to go and fly a kite.

Now I never play the giddy goat with gasbags,
And I never put the kybosh on Joe Soaps,
So I told this shicer straight, 'What, you go through the gate?
I'm a Dutchman if you do it. You? Some hopes.'

'Why don't you pop your pongo for a pony?
Or your Pip, Squeak and Wilfred you could flog.
But don't you think this gaff is Harry Freeman's
For sub-fusc spivs who sneeze at honest slog.'

'Hooky Walker!' said the Dodger. 'I've a Duchess for a tizzy
And a cherry-hog that's home on a pig's back.
But the straight wire was all guff, the gen was Dunlop duff
And the messer's mutt mazuma not jake jack.'

I've been a pukka plute since Pontius was a pilot;
I get the horrors when a rabbit's on its ribs,
So I asked the cove to join me in a noggin
Seeing as how he hadn't any decent dibs.

We sank capesmoke, snorts of mur and shots of snakejuice,
Vera Lynn, the Rosy, pimple on the rocks,
Horse's Neck, a peg of bullshot, some hoochinos,
Then he promised me that he'd pull up his socks.

It is not possible at present to publish the completely annotated translation of this work. Suffice it to say that it appears to be about an impecunious lodger who risks his last sixpence, without success, on a greyhound and is comforted by his compassionate landlord, the comfort taking the form of a prolonged drinking bout, as a result of which the lodger, somewhat improbably, resolves to mend his ways.

July 1979

Putting on the Style

It is twenty-five years since I first put on a pair of long trousers. The occasion was a visit to the Museum Hall, Bridge of Allan, to attend a presumably amateur production of a whopping melodrama entitled *Johnny Belinda*. This being an evening performance, and the subject-matter of the play—something about a deaf-mute tomboyish farm girl who becomes pregnant, as I recollect it—being, by the standards of those days, undisputably adult, shorts were in every sense, not on. I suppose that nowadays, when even three-year-olds wear jeans and not even Scouts (no longer Boy Scouts) wear shorts, the graduation to longs is no longer an event of such weighty symbolic importance as it was in the dear dead fifties. Just think of it: one day pink and time-scarred and scraped knees, the next an immaculate flannel crease from waist to ankle and the exhilarating new skill of hitching them up when you sat down in an attempt to preserve the pristine edge of that crease. Ahead lay a whole world of patent trouser-presses, steam irons and folded newspapers and, as a last resort, the business of stretching the things out last thing at night beneath the mattress, whereby the clumsy could introduce on one side an interesting pattern of bed springs. It was as much a symbol of approaching adulthood as one's first puff on a pipe, although a good deal less offensive for everyone involved.

It must have been shortly after this that I put on a dinner-jacket for the first time. While the trousers were my own, the d-j was borrowed from an older boy who cannot have been going to the dance in question. It was a proper one too, not one of those bottle-green velveteen efforts with cutaway brocade waistcoat as affected by the smarmier members of the comedian classes. It was a full-square, geometric-lapelled affair, with baggy trousers to match. It would have done credit to an elderly managing director at the firm's annual dance, but it must have looked a bit heavy on a skinny thirteen-year-old. That was the difference though: in those days one dressed to look older, whereas today one dresses to look younger. Presumably at some point one has passed oneself going in the opposite direction.

What was worn by the little girls whom we glum youths in borrowed finery pushed backwards through the quickstep and hurled bodily about in the eightsome reel now escapes me. I have a vague notion of one wearing, among other things, a voluminous petticoat with a dozen or so little bells, like those that go in a budgie's cage, sewn round the bottom, but my mind may be playing tricks.

It must have been about this time that I read a fatuous pronouncement by D. H. Lawrence to the effect that all would be well with the world when men wore red trousers (I quote from memory). That will be the day, I thought, proving myself as poor a prophet as old DH, since the next thing we knew we were in the swinging sixties, when red trousers were positively conventional and the poor old world was in no better shape than when elephant grey and heather mixture were the rage. At the time, I remember being much more impressed by Aldous Huxley's hero in *Antic Hay*, the man who while sitting on a hard chapel seat got an idea for trousers which would self-inflate.

December 1980

Distraction

You might think of me as a hack, but the designation that I prefer is 'Man of Letters'. By book-reviewing, literary journalism and the occasional bit of theatre criticism I manage to make enough to keep me in food and pen-nibs while I work on my main project, which is a biographical novel about Major Weir, the Edinburgh wizard. There is an awful lot of research to be done for a job like this, as well as an awful lot of time spent just letting information lie in one's head, being worked on by the subconscious. It's a slow business.

At the time I am talking about, I had just moved my digs to a quiet flat in a tenement in the Warrender district of Edinburgh, where I thought I would be free from distraction and able to get on with my work. I was sitting at my desk one evening looking over my notes on the Mad Major when there was a knock and my landlady put her head round the door.

'I'm just away out now,' she said. 'Hallowe'en party at the Townswomen's Guild. Would you like to come along?'

I refused, with the excuse that I had too much to do. After she had gone I sat thinking about this night and wondering what the Major would have made of dooking for apples, and treacle buns on a string. I was interrupted in my thoughts by the front door-bell ringing. When I opened the door, I was confronted by a grinning skull of light, which after the initial shock I realised was a carved turnip, held up towards me by a very pretty girl dressed in black robes and a witch's hat. Behind her stood two other girls, one dressed as a gipsy and the other in a furry cat outfit, like Puss in Boots.

'Are you not a bit old to be guising?' I said, but they just laughed.

'We're having a party down below,' said the witch girl. 'We came up to tell your landlady in case the noise disturbed her . . . would you like to come along?' she added.

So I went down the stairs with them, and into their flat, where the party was in full swing. There was a smell of incense in the air, red lights in every room, and various turnip faces like the one which had just given me the shock hanging from the walls. There were about a dozen people at the party, all dancing and singing, and occasionally breaking off to dip their faces into a huge tub of water to try to pick out an apple. I stood slightly apart to begin with, smoking a cigarette, but soon one of the girls came over to pull me into the company for an eightsome reel, then another arrived in the main room with a bowl of steaming punch and we all gathered round for a mugful. I was on my third mug, and wondering if I had spent too long avoiding the joys of company through concentrating on my book when the girl who had first spoken to me, and was then beside me, said, 'I bet you can't get an apple at the dooking.'

'What do you bet?'

'Whatever you like,' she laughed.

I went to the tub and knelt down with my hands clasped behind my back. I got my trousers rather wet on spilt water, and at one moment my spectacles fell into the tub, but I got my teeth into a huge juicy red apple and lifted it out. I looked round for the girl and saw her sitting on a sofa behind me. 'I claim a kiss,' I said boldly. She patted the sofa beside her.

'Come and sit down,' she said. I went to collect my winnings, but she held me off with a surprisingly strong hand. 'Tell me about yourself,' she said.

So I did. I told her everything I could think of, and when I had finished I said, 'Now what about you?' But she just smiled and shook her head, then as I leant forward to kiss her, she slipped under my arm, hat and all, and vanished across the room.

I didn't know whether to be annoyed or amused, so I reached for a cigarette to help me make up my mind, only to find that I had run out. I slipped out the front door, saying to someone nearby that I would be back in a moment, and ran down the three flights of stairs to the street. It took me some time to find a machine, but eventually I was running back up the stairs and knocking on the door.

It was opened by an old man in a cardigan. 'Yes?' he said.

'The party . . . ?'

'No party here.' And he shut the door.

I tried the floor down, then one up, which was my own. I tried the old man's house again, but got the same answer. Eventually, I went into my own house and lay down on my bed and thought for a long time.

My landlady has just gone off to the Townswomen's Guild party, and I am sitting here waiting for the doorbell to ring. I would not expect it to, except that on the mantelpiece, as red and round and shiny as when I first saw it, is the apple that the girl challenged me to draw from the water with my teeth.

October 1970

From the journalistic point of view it is convenient that the beginning of our period [twenty-five years earlier, when the Law Society of Scotland was founded] was dominated by the accession, on 6th February 1952, of Her Majesty the Queen and that, at the time of writing, public life is shuddering under the impact of/rejoicing in/accepting with good grace/the arrival, by various processes, of Mrs Thatcher at the top of the Tory party. It is arguable that the second could not have happened without the first. The politically unsophisticated, who think that it would be nice to have a lady Prime Minister with a grown-up family, because she would have so much to talk about when she met the Monarch, may be on to something. Likewise there is, no doubt, a sense in which they are correct who attribute Mrs Thatcher's success to an increasing willingness all round to acknowledge the claim of the Women's Liberation Movement that women are people. My suspicion, however, is that the matter goes further. Political leaders do not emerge through political merit alone; they are in addition totem animals, living embodiments of qualities which the race finds necessary in effigy if not in fact. Mrs Thatcher, I submit, is evidence of the fact that we like to be governed by women, and this in turn is but another aspect of the truth that the last twenty-five years have been woman-dominated.

May 1975

(*Mrs Thatcher became Prime Minister four years later—Editor.*)

Hearts, that Once Beat High

I was sitting shivering in the stand at Tynecastle not long ago, watching the inept efforts of Hibs to send Hearts plunging from the Premier League. 'Professionals!' said a man nearby. 'More like imposters, every one.' 'They've found Lord Lucan,' said his friend. 'He's been playing centre forward for Hearts, but nobody's noticed him.' The atmosphere was one of resigned *bonhomie*, except in one corner of the terracing, where the crowd spilled towards the attentions of the Edinburgh constabulary. 'They should tattoo "I am a football hooligan" on their foreheads,' said the man. Two policemen led out a skinny child in a thin pullover. 'I don't know what we're doing sitting here, two grown men,' said the man's friend. 'Come on and score a goal and we can go home.' Hibs's centre forward, faced with an open goal, kicked the ball high over the bar and into the thinning crowd. 'Couldn't be the centre for a doughnut,' someone said.

Both Easter Road and Tynecastle are approached through busy, shabby streets. On the terracing at Easter Road you can at least lift your eyes from the pitch and gaze at Arthur's Seat. The occasional seagull flies over from the Forth. At Tynecastle, though, there is no such sense of *rus in urbe*. High tenements hang over the ground, like the crumbling estaminets of ancient Rome. Maroon, that most miserable of colours, pervades the atmosphere. Hibs, of course, play in green. (Sydney Goodsir Smith used to say that Dundee was like Venice, in that they both had green buses.) Apart from the dreary hooligans who break the odd shop window in imbecile imitation of what they hear is done in Manchester and Millwall, no one really cares. Rome fell, Venice and Dundee decay, professional football is on its way to the wall.

Whether this is a cause for regret is hard to say. The conditions which produced the great boom in spectator sport, which sent crowds in their thousands not just to football, but to bizarre and senseless entertainments like speedway and ice hockey are by and large gone. It was a lack of sporting facilities which condemned people to spectate. Nowadays we have the facilities, easily available in most cases, although those attached to educational establishments remain incomprehensibly unused and inaccessible for much of the time. People do not need to watch, and no matter how the Scottish Football Association tinkers with its leagues and cups and blushingly flirts with commercial sponsorship they will not do so, because people have the common sense to know that it is more blessed to participate than to spectate. It is an odd paradox, of course, that so much of the finance for spectator sports comes from the manufacturers of commodities which are simply not good for your health. Presumably, by presenting their noxious product in the company of fit and healthy athletes the tobacco barons are hopeful of setting up some sort of innocence by association. Much of the responsibility for this belongs to television companies and to the curious double standards whereby Lungstopper Cigarettes may not advertise directly, but may plaster their name over racing cars and endow tournaments and competitions in the sure and certain knowledge that some vacuous commentator will repeat the name of 'Lungstopper' as long as there is breath in his body. One thing the Annan Report might have said about television is that there is far too much of it. But that's another story.

'The woods decay, the woods decay and weep' said Alfred, Lord Tennyson, who with his wholesome love of failure and falling away, would doubtless have enjoyed a chill evening at Tynecastle, watching the chimneys smoking against the evening sky and the floodlights turning the turf to an eerie green. What would that more robust enthusiast of the Heart of Midlothian, the Author of *Waverley*, have thought? No doubt he would have found something to lament in a once-proud name laid low in circumstances of commercial and urban squalor. Or perhaps he would have preferred cricket.

May 1977

[At the end of the 1987–88 season, Heart of Midlothian finished in second place in the Premier Division—Editor.]

Aesthetics and the Finance Committee

'Pertaining to the appreciation or criticism of the beautiful' was the definition of 'aesthetic', as in 'aesthetic education', offered recently to the Lothian Region Finance Committee, according to *The Scotsman*. It was but the work of a minute to track that one down to *The Shorter Oxford Dictionary*, which dates the definition at 1831. Interestingly enough, by that time the word was changing in meaning already: in 1798 it was being used, strictly, to mean 'received by the senses'; by 1871 it meant 'in accordance with good taste', whatever that might be. One difficulty about the word, in its 1831 sense, is that some ten years previously John Keats had committed himself to the proposition:

'"Beauty is truth, truth beauty,"—that is all
Ye know on earth, and all ye need to know'

a couple of lines that sound even sillier when you copy them out, but none the less admired and influential for all that. This sort of thing led in the end to the Aesthetic Movement, satirised by W. S. Gilbert in *Patience:*

'Though the Philistines may jostle, you will rank as an apostle in the high aesthetic band,
If you walk down Piccadilly with a poppy or a lily in your medieval hand.'

By the time Oscar Wilde and company were to appropriate the word to their use, it had also developed the subsidiary 1871 meaning referred to above, which might be paraphrased as 'nice' or even 'very nice'. There is a hint of this use in the somewhat sneering definition offered by *Chambers Twentieth Century Dictionary*: 'relating to possessing, or pretending to, a sense of beauty'.

All of this just goes to show how dangerous it is to try to pin down the precise meaning of the word, especially by giving an 1831 definition. Of course one does hear 'That's very aesthetic' used to mean 'That's very beautiful' or possibly, just to complicate matters, 'That's very tasteful', but since the rise of the science, or art, of aesthetics, the proper contemporary use of the word would seem to be something different. Back at the *Shorter Oxford*, we find that in the early 1800s, a German named Baumgarten ('Treegarden', if I am not mistaken) used the word to mean 'criticism of taste'. This is the most common use of the word today, although it can also be used to describe the investigation of the means whereby an artist achieves his effects.

All this said, the reason why the Committee was bending its collective mind to questions of aesthetics was to do with rating relief for the Playhouse Theatre in Edinburgh. According to *The Scotsman*, an entirely predictable discussion then took place. Someone said that if people like Billy Connolly and Andy Stewart appeared, then aesthetic education didn't come into it. Someone else replied to the effect that Billy Connolly and Andy Stewart were more fun, and made more sense, than a lot of the modern-day caterwauling that masquerades as modern art. I paraphrase, and apologise in advance if anyone has been misrepresented.

The case of Billy Connolly is an interesting one. He began as a musician, playing folk music. Presumably at that stage he would be all right aesthetically. Then the songs got shorter and the jokes got longer, so, applying Hanley's Law ('If you enjoy it, it can't be any good'), he ceased to count. Thereafter he wrote several plays, one of which, *The Red Runner*, was performed at the Traverse Theatre as part of the official Edinburgh Festival, and you can hardly get any more aesthetic than that. So far as education is concerned, involving as it does, in this context, the comparison of things incomparable, it would seem that the earnest student of the Scottish Theatre, for example, could have a highly educative time composing a thesis on, say, 'The Dichotomy of Monologue and Dialogue in the Art of William Connolly'.

A committee is, generally speaking, not a suitable instrument for achieving decisions about matters of art, and in this case one sympathises with the Committee's dilemma. Elected, in the first place, to make sure that the drains continue to work and so forth, it can hardly have expected to become involved in questions of post-Hegelian philosophy. In its difficulty, it is tempting to offer the Committee the use of an instrument called an aesthesiometer, to test acts against to see how their cultural level measures up. Unfortunately, according to *Black's Medical Dictionary*, all that that can do is measure the sensation of touch.

March 1982

The law of Scotland and the art of Scotland have this in common, that there is little else one can point at which defines our national identity. The law has a glorious tradition of supporting the Arts, though recently we have not done so much. As a relatively compact, relatively affluent, relatively cultured group of people, the lawyers of Scotland are uniquely placed to foster the Arts in an immediate and imaginative way. To give just one example, in the show of Twentieth Century Scottish Drawings, presented by STV at the Festival, there was a marvellous portrait by Alexander Moffat, a contemporary painter whose work will undoubtedly last, on sale for £90. Now, if some enterprising Faculty of Solicitors were to present that to their local art gallery. . . . There is so much that could be done, for so little cost, that would make such a contribution.

October 1976

Cameronian

Among the manifold accomplishments of the *Journal's* production editor is an ability to decipher or interpret the fine Italian hand of Petronius. Occasionally he has telephoned to elucidate a squiggle or to question a spelling, but normally he is as sound as a bell. It was with some surprise, therefore, that on casting a proprietary eye over the column recently I saw that the chap had slipped up. A casual reference to the late Norman Cameron, poet, came out as 'unjustly rejected', whereas what had been intended was 'neglected'. Neglected, rejected, what's the difference? Norman Cameron's work, it would seem, is forgotten, unconsidered and unread. This is surprising, for a number of reasons, one of the most important being that like Sir John Betjeman, although in a different way, he is an extremely good poet whose work is likely to appeal to people who do not normally read poetry.

First, though, a few biographical details. Norman Cameron was born in 1905, was educated at Fettes College and Oxford University and then went to work in Nigeria. He became friendly with Robert Graves and lived for a time near him in Majorca. Thereafter he became a copywriter with the advertising firm of J. Walter Thompson, in London. This career was interrupted by his war service, which took him to Africa and Italy. His health began to fail; in Robert Graves's words, 'In 1950 he unaccountably permitted himself to be psychoanalysed by a fellow-Scot, and soon afterwards became converted to Roman Catholicism. I have never understood the relation between these two events.' Norman Cameron died in 1953.

A poet survives through his poems and while Cameron was not prolific, it looks as though a remarkably high proportion of what he wrote is good enough to go on being read. Certainly he seems to be one of those writers to whom anthologists turn when they need something succinct, quirky and memorable. The *Collected Poems*, which are published by the Hogarth Press, the last edition being in 1967, contain fifty-seven pieces, all fairly short. Usefully, they are printed in order of composition, so that after half a dozen or so competent but not really exciting poems one comes upon the real Cameron voice in 'The Thespians at Thermopylae'. It is never easy to paraphrase a poem; with Cameron it is especially difficult because of the terse, conversational, yet allusive manner of his writing. The point of the poem is that while the courage of the Spartans at the Battle of Thermopylae has been much praised, courage was what, and all, they were good at:

'. . . numbskull courage is a kind of fear,
A fear of thought and of the oafish mothers
("Or with your shield or on it") in their rear.'

What then is one to say of the Thespians

'. . . who could see
So many roads and chose the Spartan way'?

The ironic questioning of received opinion is characteristic. It appears again, with a note of self-mockery, in 'The Compassionate Fool'. Here the narrator, invited to eat with his enemy, realises that he will be betrayed but

'. . . even as he stabbed me through and through
I pitied him for his small strategy.'

This element of self-teasing, as it were, emerges even more strongly in a quatrain, written at about the same time:

'Forgive me, Sire, for cheating your intent,
That I, who should command a regiment,
Do amble amiably here, O God,
One of the neat ones in your awkward squad.'

One of Cameron's best-known poems probably owes its celebrity in equal proportions to the skill with which it is written and the character of its subject. It is called 'The Dirty Little Accuser' and it is about his friend Dylan Thomas. Literary memoirs of the 1940s and 50s are full of accounts of the Welsh poet's drinking, scrounging way of life, but there is nothing quite as robust as the opening of Cameron's sonnet:

'Who invited him in? What was he doing here
That insolent little ruffian, that crapulous lout?
When he quitted a sofa he left a smear.
My wife says he even tried to paw her about.'

The poem goes on to say how the little lout is got rid of, but, ruefully recognising his qualities beneath the grime, concludes:

'Yet there's this check on our righteous jubilation:
Now that the little accuser is gone, of course,
We shall never be able to answer his accusation.'

One could go on quoting Cameron; perhaps that is one of the attractions of his writing, that at a time when many of his contemporaries were reaching in their sack of apocalyptic symbols, he continued to believe that it was possible to write clearly what you meant to say. One final, lighter example shows this:

'When you confess your sins before a parson,
You find it no great effort to disclose
Your crimes of murder, bigamy and arson,
But can you tell him that you pick your nose?'

Cameron's experiences in Africa produced what many of his readers would agree to be his masterpiece, a poem, slightly longer than usual, about a journey by truck across the desert to a town where there was fresh water. It is too much of an entity to permit quotation. It is entitled 'Green, Green is El Aghir' and is worth searching out.

Perhaps the last word, for the moment, can be left to Robert Graves, who expressed himself with an economy with which his subject would have approved: 'When, in my more intolerant days, people would ask me crossly: "All right, if you think So-and-so and So-and-so and So-and-so are no good as poets, who *is* any good?", I used to answer, "Why, for a start, there's Norman Cameron."'

July 1981

Good Scout

While clearing out a cupboard recently, I found a chunky yellow volume, somewhat tattered, that must have been lying there for close on thirty years. Dear me, or 'expletive deleted', I thought, is it as long as that since I put aside the woggle and the toggle, the broad-brimmed hat and the belt with the funny buckle? Correct, dear reader, what I had found was *Scouting for Boys*, handbook of innocence.

It is tempting to flesh out this piece with copious quotation: B-P's enthusiastic, optimistic style certainly invites it ('It may be that some day one of you will be the first person to find a dead body . . .') but it is a temptation that must be resisted, since the book has now been passed on to younger and more Scoutish hands. I'm not even certain about the above quotation, which is from memory.

B-P's attitude to smoking and drinking was notorious: he was against both since it made it harder to detect (presumably by smelling) a hidden enemy. That the lurking assassin might be lured out of concealment by craftily leaving a half-bottle of Bell's and ten Senior Service under a convenient palm-tree does not seem to have occurred to him. He does, however, seem to realise that his abolitionist arguments may be less than convincing to young chaps, for he bolstered his position with a glance at more delicate matters. What, in some circumstances, is to be stigmatised as 'beastliness' (brought on, *inter alia*, by constipation and over-indulgence in rich foods—so much for 'oysters is amorous') can, viewed in another light, be OK. Girls, or rather young women, we are told, are likely to put off the chap whose breath reeks of the brewery and the tobacconist's. Whether this advice stands up today, or whether it is the fellow with the tang of glue on his lips or the smattering of cocaine dust around his reddened nostrils who is unlikely to make first base, it would take a modern B-P, opinionated, inquiring and out of touch, to decide.

Lest the following be construed as some sort of attack on the World Wide Fellowship, let me say at once just this. . . . Oh, I've forgotten what I was going to say. So much for those solitary hours knocking-up at Kim's Game (ingredients, in case you don't remember, a tray, a cloth and a number of objects to cover, uncover, view, cover and recall). Ah, yes, what I was going to say was it's amazing how much of the stuff one remembers. Dig a little hole beside the tent-pole, so that if it rains in the night it can be moved, thus instantly slackening all of the guy ropes. A Scout is Clean in Thought, Word and Deed—the last two certainly, but the first one is a bit difficult to control, surely. Wasn't there something about Smiling and Whistling at All Times? Perhaps it's in that little piece of instruction that a clue to one's slight dismay at the Movement's endless, boundless optimism is to be found. It's not, I think, that Scouting was racist, although in its time it probably was imperialist, nor that it is so determinedly middle-class in its values, but it is in its belief that the darker side of life could be banished if a fellow kept his bowels open and his mind closed that the weakness of the idea, which is the weakness of simplicity, lies.

That said, it is difficult not to look back through the bleary eye of nostalgia to some of the pleasures of those days—to the chap who, in order to win some badges, dismantled and remantled, if that is the word, his bicycle, only to find that it worked with several unallocated parts left over, to the awful heartburn brought on by a mixture of half-cooked stew-and-ashes (the billycan fell over and put the fire out and we were too hungry to wait), to the enormous pleasure of not hiking any longer—those who have done it will not forget it.

The troop to which I belonged, briefly, was small (Eagles, Curlews and, surely it can't have been, Coots) and for small, pre-boarding-school boys. Snatched away in early adolescence from the pleasures of the bowline and the fear of hoisting the flag upside down, we were spared the torments of older Scouts, of shaving in camp and of the temptation to close encounters with Girl Guide troops. Although short in time, the experience of the world of B-P may be long in significance and perhaps that is why the book at the back of the cupboard brought it all back. Anyway, have you done *your* good deed for the day?

April 1982

Received ideas

Damson
The national fruit of Scotland.
    'Comely, wersh, o' purpie hue,
    Wee plum of Alba, we eat you'—H. MacDiarmid.

Dentists
They make a fortune early in life, but once their wrists and ankles go they usually end up eking out a living as property speculators. Seldom marry their receptionists.

Dictaphone
That infernal machine which along with the telephone has ruined the prose style of two generations. See 'Off-the-cuff judgements, mastery'.

January 1987

Handy Hints for the Man of Letters

The practice of literary criticism is sometimes considered to be the proper prerogative of the expert, of the likes of F. R. Leavis, if he had a like, although anyone who could describe *The House with the Green Shutters* as being in the tradition of *Wuthering Heights* would seem to find his place more in the history of the building trade than that of art. The most extreme remove from this cloistered academicism is the celebrity as arbiter of taste: *Kevin Keegan Looks at the Burrell Collection*, for instance, or *Cilla Black's T. S. Eliot Fireside Book*. What has become of the man of letters, I am asked, that fellow with the well-rounded grasp, the wide, if shallow, range, the mellifluous phrase and the apposite anecdote? The answer, it is suggested, is in the hands of the inquirer. Here follows a set of rules whereby anyone can be his own man of letters. Be your ambition the humble 'Armchair Pipeman' column in *The Nicotine Traders' Gazette*, or the book pages of the very *Jocksman* itself, here are some rules to follow.

1   Pedantry has its place. The correct mode is sorrow rather than anger: 'It seems odd that a writer of Mr Sheep's distinction should confuse "parameter" with "perimeter".' A little more irritation can be permitted in order to correct the publisher as well as the author: 'Alas, Mr Goat has been badly served by his proof-readers, who allow him to commit himself to the evidently absurd proposition that the Battle of Bannockburn was fought not long after that of Agincourt.'

2   Personal knowledge is invaluable. Commonly known as 'name-dropping', this can be employed in two ways. First, there is the name-drop general: 'Tyrone Guthrie once remarked to me, as we walked through the orchard at Château-le-Gaz, that the leaf told us more about the tree than the tree about the leaf. This conversation came back to me, agreeably, as I read with much pleasure Bruno Pig's new collection of essays on the theatre, *Chekhov and Chips*.' Secondly, there is the name-drop particular, where the reviewer has, or pretends to have, some particular knowledge of the matter in hand: 'Although Mr Fox records, quite correctly, Galsworthy's oft-expressed public admiration of Oscar Wilde, it would be wrong of me to let this moment pass without recording that on the last occasion when we dined together Jack referred, bitterly and frequently, to the Irish "wit" as a blabber-mouthed old ponce who would have had trouble getting a job in the epigrams department of a Birmingham cracker-factory.'

3   The comparison of false similarities is one way of keeping the piece rolling along: 'Turning to Arthur Hen's new novella, *Springtime in the Hatshop*, one looks for the blood-and-thunder, the sense of almost molten *Weltschmerz* that one found in the recently published *Grotto of Destiny* by Herr Hen's distinguished compatriot, Frau Lucy Horse, but alas! one looks in vain.'

4   Criticism of omissions as to matters of fact is another way of demonstrating effortless superiority: 'I find it astonishing that so eminent a scholar as Dr Stoat should go for his sources to the traditionally derivative manuscript in Trinity College Library when, as has been known at least since the researches of Sir Weasel Rabbit, a more persuasive reading is to be found in the Codex II held by the Tretchikov Museum and available to scholars since 1968.'

5   A version of the above, when one has nothing useful to add, is the extended agreement: 'Prof Polecat's account of the incident at Glastonbury when Virginia Woolf broke a tooth on a mince pie which Duncan Grant had absent-mindedly allowed to remain under the grill longer than he should have (the so-called "Alfred Incident") does not differ substantially from that given to me by V. Sackville-West when we lunched with Cyril Connolly at the Ferrets in the autumn of 1936.'

6   It is useful to examine in detail each text, or at least part thereof. A look at the opening paragraph of this piece, for

example, will reveal one or two handy little devices. It begins with the statement general (and thus virtually meaningless). The remark about F. R. Leavis, deceased and thus unable to reply, is an example of the wounding thrust *post mortem*. The reference to his remark about *The House with the Green Shutters*, although perhaps indicating a wide acquaintance with the works of the sage, might in fact be based on no more than a narrow acquaintance with the introduction to the Holmes McDougall edition of the novel in question. The somewhat clumsy joke about builders is intended to be an in-joke based on Leavis's remark about Edith Sitwell belonging to the history not of poetry but of publicity.

Other, more rarefied hints could be given, on such matters as apt quotations from foreign tongues, or when it is advisable to employ the joke risqué, but even the most maladroit conjurer must keep something up his ragged sleeve. In any case, the final tip is that the reader should always be left believing that he, like the author under review, knows at least a little less than the humble reviewer.

May 1982

Received ideas

Wilson's Phalarope
The music-hall-cum-circus, situated in a tent on Glasgow Green, 1890 to 1910, was a popular meeting-place for courting couples in our grandparents' time. 'Meet me at the Phalarope,' sang Gertie Gitana, 'and I will give you cause to hope.' Closed after the Great Clyde Flood of 1910, which had urchins singing, 'And bring along a bar of soap.'

Woody Nightshade
American stand-up comedian arrested at Prestwick for possession of illegal substances. Originator of the sentence 'I've learned my lesson now and would like to do something for the kids to keep them from getting into this sort of trouble'. Last heard of defending a palimony suit in Atlantic City on the grounds of temporary insanity, ie, *pro tem* his head did not know where it was at.

June 1986

The Living Dead

There was a suggestion in the *Lancet* recently that doctors might be encouraged to write their own obituaries. The idea behind the scheme was that from their new position amid the Great Majority, distinguished medical men would feel free to express themselves without fear or favour, while at the same time we would be spared the inaccurate effusions, whether inspired by unction or malice, of those they left behind. Would it work for lawyers, though? Here are a few trial runs, obligingly dashed off by columnar correspondents.

1   Cornelius Humph passed advocate in 1937, having devilled to Archibald Egg (later Lord Egg), a master whose legal knowledge he came to distrust almost as much as he despised his eating habits. Humph's deep-seated learning, broad experience of life and profound humanity failed to win him the extensive practice generally predicted for him by his wide circle of friends and it was with some relief that he accepted the appointment of sheriff substitute of Volta and Upper Amazon. At the dinner given by the local faculty of procurators to celebrate his fifty years in this office, he confessed that he could not now recall the details of a single case which he had heard during that time, an assertion that his audience was only too willing to credit. Shortly after his passing advocate, Sheriff Humph married Verbena, older daughter of Fergus Ferguson, Esq, WS, who later declined to follow him on his appointment, preferring to continue her life in Edinburgh. Their union was not blessed with issue.

2   V. Duff, Solicitor, spent the first years of his legal life with the firm of Haddock & Skink, Advocates in Aberdeen, where he early developed an aptitude for avoiding the cashier, talking to typists and taking the senior partner's dog for a walk. Seeking to widen his experience he moved to the firm of Goodfun & Jolly, SSC, Edinburgh, where he was soon assumed partner. Shortly after his first Court of Session jury trial, when he inadvertently omitted to fee-fund the jury precept, he took up a position in the public service and enjoyed a distinguished career which culminated in his retiral at the age of eighty-six from the position of Clerk of the Trustees of Skinktoun Harbour. In 1932 he published a short monograph, 'Some Thoughts on the Proposed Abolition of the Civil Jury Trial' (*Proceedings of the Society of Clerks to Harbour Trustees and Clerks to Water Boards of North East Scotland*, Vol 23). In an interview published in the *Skinktoun Bugler* on the occasion of his retiral he gave his hobbies as fiddle music and law reform.

3   B. F. Right-Placeman was educated at Edinburgh Academy; Trinity College, Oxford; Caius College, Cambridge; Edinburgh University and the Sorbonne. His unusual distinction in being educated at both southern universities was the result, in part, of what he liked to describe as 'an altercation' late at night and towards the end of his first year, with the châtelaine of Lady Margaret Hall, then a women's college. Family influence (his uncle was at the time Provost of Eton College) secured him a place at Caius, where he rowed with distinction in the College boat. After a period at Edinburgh (his ascent of the north face of the Scott Monument is still spoken of) he expressed a wish to abandon the study of law for that of letters. An indulgent father permitted him two years in Paris: the Paris of Joyce, Fitzgerald, Hemingway and Picasso, none of whom he met. After seeing through the press his short collection of lyrics *Lasses of Isis and Cam*, he returned to Edinburgh and the bar, becoming successfully Session Cases Reporter, Collector of the Advocates' Widows' Fund, Sheriff Court Depute and Vice-Dean. He stood unsuccessfully, to his relief, for Falkirk Burgh in the 1948 by-election. Latterly, many a bar dinner was enlivened by his high-spirited renditions of satirical verses of his own devising. His frequently reiterated claim that he received no instructions at all during the three years after he took silk was scarcely an exaggeration, although his net income steadily increased through his wise stewardship of his wife's investments.

4   Arthur Gravy, Solicitor, 'Father of the Glasgow Bar' as he liked to call himself, came from a legal family only to the extent that his revered father regularly suffered the indignity of civil imprisonment for debt. Arthur's characteristically modest courtroom style ("No law is trite to me, M'Lud," he once remarked), together with a constitution weakened by an early upbringing in damp lodgings and a voice which, though often pertinent, was seldom forceful, meant that many, to their peril, underestimated his forensic ability. His cross-examination of the defender in the case of *Maxie's Kebabs* v *Cumbernauld Cat Refuge* is still spoken of. It was his misfortune in the later case to see a verdict which he had won in the sheriff court being lost in the Division by an ill-prepared junior counsel who thought that he knew better than his instructing agents. Mr Gravy was often to be seen in the library of the Faculty of Procurators, where he claimed to go for a free heat in the years following his single and catastrophic venture into property development. A trophy presented by him to his old university to be awarded for the best essay on the law of teinds is still competed for. His dislike of the introduction of allegedly humorous articles into serious legal journals was notorious.

February 1983

In William J. Tait's collected poems, *A Day Between Weathers*, there is 'Barcelona Boond—A Glesca Haiku':

'Knoack'n it back abuin the cloods, an aa
Yon Fenian Wogs tae bash yet . . . Jings!'

October 1980

People's Palaces

Abbotsford, Kenilworth, Waverley. This is not an essay on Sir Walter Scott, however, but a reference to three attractive public houses, brought on in part by the pleasantly thirst-making weather at the time of writing though owing more to the recent publication of a most handsome book. *People's Palaces* by Rudolph Kenna and Anthony Mooney is a labour of love; more to the point it is a celebration of the golden age of the Scottish pub, of the splendid Victorian and Edwardian buildings which, with luck, even today have not been obliterated by the brewers' obsession with turning pubs into sanctuaries for Space Invaders, plastic cheese and fizzy beer.

Much recent writing on pubs and pub-goers, exemplified, for instance, by Richard Boston, whom God preserve, in his excellent *Beer and Skittles*, has been CAMRA-esque. The theme here was essentially a consumer one: what Boston objected to was not people drinking keg beer or lager, it was that economies of scale were being used to diminish the choice available to the customer. CAMRA's triumph, the advance of the Real Ale movement, is essentially to have given back a measure of freedom to drinkers who were being offered a reducing, and to them increasingly unacceptable, range of beers.

Messrs Kenna and Mooney may well be CAMRAmen: certainly they have the true enthusiasts' ability to mix information and entertainment. Their subject, however, is a different one, no less than a social history of urban Scotland seen through a glass—darkly if necessary, for they do not ignore the misery too often associated with alcohol.

The authors begin by giving us a highly readable sketch of the ancestry of the Scottish pub. We are taken through the taverns frequented by the Edinburgh literati—Hume, Raeburn, Fergusson, Burns—where, among others, we meet James Boswell: 'I went to Fortune's; found nobody but Captain James Gordon of Ellon. He and I drank five bottles of claret and were most profound politicians.' We are shown, too, the taverns of Glasgow, with their cock-pits and rat-pits; the Zebra in the High Street, where sparring was the rage, and the singing-houses, rudimentary music-halls clustered in the closes of the Saltmarket. Jolly as these places may have been, there seems little doubt that until the 1850s at least they were, architecturally, on the squalid side. Women seldom were to be seen.

What drink was taken in the pubs of yesteryear? At the beginning of the nineteenth century, the taste was for old, heavy beers. The evolution of lighter beers followed. By the early 1900s Edinburgh had thirty-five breweries, and Alloa had eight (to a population of 11,000), mostly producing lighter, drier beers on the lines of India Pale Ale. The nineteenth century also saw the whisky boom, a story in itself, with Aeneas Coffey's patent still of 1830 producing the stuff in huge quantities and the entrepreneurial efforts of Buchanan and Dewar almost literally pouring it down people's throats. Some of the stuff on offer was pretty crude and among the solutions available to the problem of the rawness of grain spirit was Maturite, a few drops of which imparted 'such mellow and palatable properties that, while its potency and strength were retained, it was pleasant to the taste and smelled as old malt'.

The main and most important purpose of the book, however, is not the discussion of who drank what but of where they drank it. The book is profusely illustrated with photographs of gantries, horseshoe bars, dados, pillars, stained glass—of all the details that made these pubs such interesting places. We are not likely to see their equal for, as the authors say, 'Their characteristic features would be extremely expensive to reproduce today; craftsmen are no longer a prolific breed and their work now commands respect in terms of hard cash.' Elsewhere the authors say, 'The palace pubs were products of an age brimming with self-confidence, low taxation and abundant craftsmanship—a fortuitous combination which in all probability will never occur again.' It has to be added that an appreciation of the value of these places as works of art and architecture has come almost, if not actually, too late. Many have been demolished or modernised. Even as late as 1969 The Café Royal in Edinburgh, probably the single finest building of its kind, an opulent classic of *fin de siècle* decoration, was threatened with demolition to make way for an extension to a chain-store.

This is a book that will appeal to anyone interested in social history, architecture, drink—all or any of the three. For the lawyer, there is in addition an intelligent and informed discussion of the historical basis of our licensing laws. Also for the lawyer there is a reminder of how much of value to the historian may lurk among those old deeds that somehow never got thrown out. Sederunt and minute books, trust dispositions and settlements and inventories and valuations from solicitors' records deposited in the Strathclyde Regional Archives provided the authors with much useful material. Something worth looking into, perhaps?

July 1983

Every age produces its own appropriate art form, and clearly opera, or at any rate grand opera, is not the form of our day. In style and in content it is far too extravagant, and this extravagance is organic and cannot be separated from the thing. The avowed purpose of those who originally demanded, and by paying for it thus effectively created grand opera, was conspicuous consumption. But because the promoters of the Suez Canal, for example, felt able to advertise its opening by commissioning an expensive, unbalanced monster like *Aida*, is there any reason why the hapless taxpayer should continue to prop up the pyramids?

August 1974

Wally's Wha Haes

The following document blew in the window a few days ago and landed on the Petronian desk. It was headed 'Not for immediate publication', but as a few days have passed it should be all right.

Scots to send Eleven only to Mexico

The SFA, in a shock announcement today, stated that, due to cuts, the World Cup Party would be limited to eleven. The team, with our special correspondent's comments, is:

Goal: Walter Scott. Aptly-named skipper Wally with his huge hands (his gloves can be inspected at Abbotsford) is an inspired custodian and dashing leader. He spent his career with Heart of Midlothian and now comes out of retirement to lead the team. Hobbies include building mock-gothic houses.

Right back: Gavin Douglas. A surprise choice, Gavin is the first bishop to win a cap. Currently with unfashionable Dunkeld, the selectors have obviously not forgotten his part in the club's recent VIII–I thrashing of Bath and Wells to take the Diocesan Challenge Trophy. When not carrying out his duties as a prelate, Gavin relaxes by translating the *Aeneid* into aureate Scots.

Left back: James Hogg. 'The Electric Shepherd' was born in rugby country but has made his mark with Hibs, where his split personality goes virtually unnoticed. A stolid defender, Jim is capable of flights of fancy which can baffle his team-mates and he has been known to put the odd own goal past his great pal, keeper Wally.

Right half: George Gordon. Technically an Anglo, Geordie ('Byron' to his friends), remains true to his Aberdeen roots. His local patriotism and a liking for the ladies have earned him the nickname of 'Don Juan' on the terraces. The sort of arrogant schemer who can make a team tick, there remain serious doubts about his physical, and moral, fitness.

Centre half: Thomas the Rhymer. A real surprise choice this, Tommy hasn't been seen in his usual haunts for seven years. I've been told in Melrose that he has been transported to the gaiety of faerieland (though this might have been 'transferred to Gala Fairydean'). His inclusion depends, it is supposed, on his own prophecy:

'Tide by tide, whate'er betide,
Tom will make the Mexico side.'

Left half: R. L. Stevenson. Louis's frail exterior belies the tough tackler who learned his trade at the feet (or foot) of Long John Silver. Experience picked up in his nocturnal forays round the top of Leith Walk should ensure that he can take care of himself when the *señors'* boots start swinging. Veteran of many overseas tours, he usually travels with a donkey.

Right wing: Thomas Carlyle. Tom's political views make this position his own. His Superman philosophy often leads to the Expatriate from Ecclefechan trying too much on his own, but his tendency to public denunciation of his team-mates is made up for by his capacity for sheer graft. His recent marriage to Haddington beauty queen Jane Welsh has not affected his training.

Inside right: James Barrie. The original Scotsman on the make, Jim's apparently eternal youth and native tenacity have surprised a good few who didn't expect such a lot from a small chap. The Kirriemuir Ballplayer was knighted not long ago and is believed to be the inventor of the name 'Wendy'. He is unmarried and lives with a photograph of his mother.

Centre forward: Robert Burns. Rab, the people's choice, first caught the eye when transferred to Edina from Tarbolton Boys Club. A dashing and popular leader of the line, he has had his difficulties with training schedules, but his natural grace and wit make him incomparable. Hobbies are fornication and repentance.

Inside left: James Bridie. 'Doc', as he is known, is a true expert on the commission and treatment of the professional foul. Somewhat given to glittering, mazy beginnings which somehow tail off, Doc will have to work on his stamina at altitude, most of his successful performances having taken place in London's West End.

Outside left: Hugh MacDiarmid. 'Chris', another battling Borderer, can confuse the opposition by suddenly appearing to pop up on the right for a spell, although always being able to assure his team-mates after the game that such a thing never happened. A player of huge courage and skill, it is to be hoped that he will stick to his place on the field and not resign to join the Mexican government in exile or plot to bring down the Tijuana branch of PEN. Hobby: Anglophobia.

These are the men then who carry our hopes across the Atlantic. When shall we see their like again? (c The Corries.)

March 1986

Lord Denning, *The Family Story* (Butterworths). Lord Denning's prose style is famous: in many a sentence he dispenses with the verb. Nouns and adjectives. Expressive and simple but slightly unnerving. But that is his way. Infectious too. One brother became a general. Another an admiral. Tom rose to the very top and was widely loved personally, his decisions sometimes less so. Wrongly. This moving and profound account of a life led on its own terms is sentenced to go on being read. Good day to you.

November 1985

Correspondence Course

When social historians come to judge our century and all the appalling things that have happened in it, one wonders if they will have time or opportunity to consider the way that we might have lived, as exemplified by a fat volume, *The News Chronicle Enquire Within*, published not long after George VI took the throne and containing, according to its editor, 1,500,000 words (of text)—well worth the 20p that it went for recently.

Apart from tips about how to enamel a bath and as to the correct time for stocking an aviary, the information that great explorers often have a mole on their noses and a telling piece on the best way to go about testing an Axminster carpet, the 'Library of Information' includes an indispensable section on letter-writing.

The novel in letter form has an honourable history. Sometimes this treatment can be on the tedious side, but as a means of conveying what characters felt about one another, or pretended to, it can scarcely be bettered. The form reached its zenith in *Les Liaisons Dangereuses* by Leclos, an astonishing book in which the corrupt write letters about what they are going to do to the innocent and the innocent write letters about not knowing what is going on. The form faded away in the face of the exemplary narrative brilliance of Thackeray and Dickens, but it is interesting to see that it has been revived by the Sage of Byres Road, Alasdair Gray, to brilliant effect, in *Unlikely Stories, Mostly*.

In the *News Chronicle* book, the compiler of the 'Social Letter Writer' ('model letters for home and social purposes') has written a modern masterpiece in this most difficult of forms. After some tendentious stuff about the use of the apostrophe and when to use postcards ('It is the height of bad form and taste to write an unpleasant remark about a third person on a postcard') we are plunged into the difficult business of refusing invitations to children's parties ('Baby is suffering from a mild attack of whooping cough'), dances ('We have an engagement that evening to dine with friends at Muddleford'), and tea parties ('Speech Day Celebrations at Walter's school'). It becomes apparent that the point of replying at all is to establish one's social superiority to the hapless invitor ('Walter will not be able to come as he has been selected to play cricket with the First XI'). In spite of this, relations seem to improve and an invitation to stay is extended by the Twiggs (as they sign themselves). The Longs seem eager to go, but 'my husband's mother is very sadly indeed and has the doctor in close attendance'. Never mind. The Twiggs send out a stream of invitations to a wedding, a coming-of-age in the British Legion Hall and a christening.

Next in this saga of relationships we come upon Cynthia Long expressing her regret that 'little Ethel has passed away in the Cottage Hospital'. The editor informs us that 'florists who supply wreaths are usually prepared to supply black-edged cards'. Life has to go on though and soon once again we are up and running. The Longs go to stay with the Twiggs ('We liked your friends in the adjoining house immensely. . . . Sam is still talking about his fishing experience with Mr Twiggs' (ho hum)) and then suddenly people start getting married ('The beautiful brass dinner gong you so kindly sent us').

Thereafter this union is blessed with issue. Letters pour in from people wishing to 'see the little chap', but before we know where we are he has passed an examination successfully and involved himself in a nasty incident with a neighbour ('Our cat was struck yesterday with a pellet from an airgun . . . two large panes in our glass conservatory . . .'). Ignoring such incidents as the one in which Mrs Long attributes her son's absence from school to her husband's wish that he should attend his niece's wedding, we are soon back with romance. Harry proposes in writing and Agnes replies, variously. 'Say you'll be my own sweet darling wife' elicits the response, 'Yes' ('Do you really want to call me "wifie" for ever and always?') and 'No' ('I have always seen in you a loyal and staunch comrade and pal'). The subtlety of the chap's note to the girl's parents ('I dare say that you have noticed for a long time that Agnes and I have been spending a lot of time together') scarcely seems to merit the reply, 'If you care to work, however, with greater application than is now apparent . . . you may approach the matter again when she is twenty-one.'

Worse could happen, though, to a paterfamilias ('. . . made it your business to intrude upon her most persistently during her homeward journeys from the office'), but no sooner has love found a way than comes the tiff. 'After you jumped on the bus last evening and went home alone, leaving me with my own wretched thoughts', prompts the response, 'You were not the only one who was unhappy last night.'

Troubles don't come singly, though. He is forced to write, 'You seemed to spend all the time with Florrie Wilkinson, and to have practically none to spare for me.' She replies, 'You used to play tennis with me every weekend but now you have taken up cricket instead. You appear to prefer motoring with the Wilkinsons to taking walks with me. Shall I send you back your ring?'

And there, unfortunately, it ends. There follows a plethora of worthy information about mortise and tenon joints, raising half-hardy annuals and the answer to the question 'Who invented the tricycle?' While one may be cheered to know that Kilmarnock is a splendid tourist centre and that Montrose possesses many quaint houses, the questions abide—what became of the Twiggs and their social pretensions; of the Longs and their polite refusals; of Agnes and Harry, hopelessly confused about their feelings for one another? Did anyone lay a flower on the grave of little Ethel? What ever happened to all of these people who had to get someone else to write their letters for them?

July 1985

Lucy

Several years ago I spent a weekend with friends in their fortified house on the East March of the Border, not far from Duns. I was to play for the home team: the opposition (although that is far too hard a word) was a man from Malta whom we will call Tony, since that is his name. He was an invited but unknown guest. His whole passion in life was Donizetti's opera *Lucia di Lammermoor* and he had come to Scotland to see its setting for himself. Discovering that the house in question was said to be Ravenswood (Scott having moved it a few miles), he telephoned to ask if he could have a look round. With the exuberant generosity which their friends have come to expect of them, the family invited him to stay.

Private occasions are not for public consumption, so it is sufficient to say that Tony, who eventually left with a stone from the garden among his souvenirs, delighted and slightly shamed us with his enthusiasm. What do you say to someone who has seen the opera more than a hundred times and heard the recording more than a thousand? At long last, and with some diffidence, I read the book the other day, and I say 'day' advisedly, because *The Bride of Lammermoor* is unputdownable.

It is, curiously, only as a writer that the Wizard of the North has gone out of fashion; his statue, Scotland's granite moonshot, still sits on Princes Street; Heart of Midlothian are not yet Atletico Double Glazing; bus-borne illiterates still troop through Abbotsford (at least visitors to Graceland buy Elvis's records!). Thus Scott is treated as a phenomenon of nature: we are not in the position of his first readers, for whom Henry Cockburn spoke when he wrote '. . . the unexpected newness of the thing . . . struck me with an electric shock of delight'. We now take for granted what he said first. After all, if a man invents the historical novel, Southern Chivalry and the Trossachs, the country we inhabit is largely of his invention. As Jorge Luis Borges says in his story 'Pierre Menard', *Don Quixote* written by someone else this century would be a different book even if the words were the same.

To read Scott comfortably it is advisable to be prepared to skip, particularly where descriptive writing is concerned, and to go back if necessary. The point is that many of Scott's readers could no more hope to see, say, Fast Castle than the other side of the moon. We who can do so without winding down the window of our Ford Fiesta are differently situated. This is not to say that descriptions are to be avoided: the view of the city from the Wicks o'Baiglie, for example, which opens *The Fair Maid of Perth* is a model of witty and lucid scene-setting, and in *Lammermoor* the country itself, though more wild and unforgiving than it seems today, is virtually a character.

One of the reasons for the decline of Scott in popular favour is that ours is an age that, thanks to Freud, greatly values the neurotic. This is not necessarily wrong, but it does mean that James Hogg is preferred not for the broad political comedy of 'The Edinburgh Baillie' but for the sulphurous pathology of *The Confessions of a Justified Sinner*, or R. L. Stevenson for the unfinished, and unbalanced, *Weir of Hermiston* rather than for the cunningly achieved *Kidnapped*. While one would like to enter a plea for the works of broad sanity and social and political reconciliation, here it must be admitted that *Lammermoor* is Scott's morbid masterpiece.

At the time of its composition, Scott was very ill and, in fact, dictated it to two amanuenses. As he was too ill to correct the proofs, the first he saw of it in print was as a finished book. He read it with some trepidation since, as he told James Ballantyne, he 'did not recall a single incident, character or conversation which it contained'. This must have been alarming to him. His verdict on reading the book? 'I felt it monstrous gross and grotesque: but the worst of it made me laugh, and I trusted the good-natured public would not be less indulgent.' Pressed by a reader with the suggestion that Caleb Balderstone, the proud and self-deluding old family retainer whose insistence on past glories is one of the principal plotting devices, is a caricature, Scott agreed that 'he might have sprinkled rather too much parsley over his chicken'.

The broad story of the book may be summarised thus. Edgar, a Byronic chap, falls for Lucy Ashton, whose family live in his ancestral home. Unfortunately he believes that Lucy's father is the man responsible for his own father's ruin. His rival for Lucy's hand, though not her love, is Bucklaw, oafish but decent, the sort of chap who might go to agricultural college because he is too stupid to get into the Navy. Edgar (same name, curiously, as the bastard in *King Lear*) has to go abroad for the Old Cause. If he is not back by the appointed day, Lucy must marry Bucklaw, something nobody, except the real villain who is motivated only by malice, wishes to happen.

One very odd thing about the book is the presence in it of the supernatural. There are prophecies, promises of revenge, ravens slain, philosophical sextons and so forth, but never once does one feel that they are being used as stage props. That this should be so has puzzled some commentators, who have felt that Scott was simply tarting up his story with unnecessary Gothic accoutrements. The answer, I believe, is not so obvious. It is that Scott, who knew and loved the Border Ballads, with his mind made less deliberate by his enervating sickness, achieved something of that blend of the mundane and the otherworldly that is to be found in ballads like 'The Wife of Usher's Well', 'The Unquiet Grave' and 'Thomas the Rhymer'. Men and women have been credited with unearthly powers simply because they are more observant and more sensitive than their fellows: Scott, it might be said, regarded magic as lost knowledge and this may be why, in the famous story, he turned aside and wept as he walked down the Mound at the damage done by reformers who do not realise that change means loss.

To say more would be to say too much, but potential readers might be interested to know that Lucy's story is based on that of the daughter of none other than Lord President Stair.

September 1987

It has been a pleasure to gather the thoughts and sensations of the previous month and to try to present them in some sort of order, both for the sake of doing it and in the hope that sometimes an enthusiasm can be shared and an enjoyment recorded. That most readable of critics, Cyril Connolly, wrote in the introduction to his selected essays, *Previous Convictions:* 'If I have a gift, it is that of being able to communicate my enthusiasm for literature and throw a little light on my favourite authors.' Not a bad motto.

October 1976